SOUP CLUB MANIFESTO
A DECLARATION OF FOOD SHARING

We declare that soup shall be **SHARED**.

Why soup? Soup scales up and **TRAVELS** well.

Soup is economical, basic, and **NONDENOMINATIONAL**.

Soup Club is **A STATE OF BEING**, not a monthly meeting.

We are not limited to **SPECIAL OCCASION** soup
for holidays, births, moving, or grief.

The **MAGICAL DELIVERY** of soup to your door
is elemental to Soup Club.

SALT your soup. Embrace crushed red pepper.

A black belt is a white belt who **NEVER QUIT**. Make your soup.

NEVER APOLOGIZE for your soup.

Make soup with **ABANDON**.

Remember, it's just **SOUP**.

You will need a bigger pot.

THE SOUP CLUB COOKBOOK

FEED YOUR FRIENDS.
FEED YOUR FAMILY.
FEED YOURSELF.

Courtney Allison, Tina Carr,
Caroline Laskow & Julie Peacock

PHOTOGRAPHS BY ANNIE SCHLECHTER ◆ ILLUSTRATIONS BY KATE NECKEL

CLARKSON POTTER/PUBLISHERS

NEW YORK

Published in the United States by Clarkson Potter/Publishers,
an imprint of the Crown Publishing Group,
a division of Random House LLC,
a Penguin Random House Company, New York.
www.crownpublishing.com
www.clarksonpotter.com

CLARKSON POTTER is a trademark and POTTER with
colophon is a registered trademark of Random House LLC.

Library of Congress Cataloging-in-Publication Data
Allison, Courtney
The soup club cookbook: feed your friends, feed your family,
feed yourself / Courtney Allison [and 3 others].
1. Soups. 2. One-dish meals. I. Title.
TX757.A48   2014
641.81'3—dc23   2014009496

ISBN 978-0-7704-3462-5
eBook ISBN 978-0-7704-3463-2

Printed in China

Book design by Laura Palese
Cover design by Rae Ann Spitzenberger
Cover photographs by Annie Schlechter

1 2 3 4 5 6 7 8 9 10

First Edition

**THIS BOOK IS DEDICATED
TO OUR MOTHERS:**

Sarah, Kirsten, Nancy, and Karen;
for all they have given us,
including (but not limited to) soup.

CONTENTS

PART THREE

FOOD FOR FORKS & FINGERS
149

INTRODUCTION

*It began as a conversation. We missed each other
but couldn't always eat together. So we started a club:*

WE GREW UP IN OTHER PLACES and settled in New York City, sacrificing thousands of square feet in personal living space in exchange for diversity and density, great art, cheap manicures, access to truly hot peppers, public transportation, and very old tenements that have bars with killer cocktails.

We are an educator, an ecologist, a filmmaker, a nutritionist, a yogi, a traveler, a feminist, a mother, a runner, a Dane, a Jew, a Yankee, a Christian, a vegetarian, a gardener, and a coffee drinker.

We make sure each other's glasses are filled with seltzer or wine, as the case may be. We pick up, hang on to, feed, and hug each other's kids with abandon. We try to be honest and kind and sometimes succeed at doing both.

We are four friends who cook and we are Soup Club.

○ ○ ○ ○ ○ ○ ○ ○ ○ ○ ○ ○ ○ ○ ○ ○ ○ ○

What we do is simple: We take turns cooking big pots of soup, enough to feed our four families. We drop off the soup, along with sides and garnishes, at the homes of our three other club members. This happens once a week, which means that we each cook our big pot of soup once a month. The other three weeks, we are treated to one another's home cooking. This book is the product of our actual Soup Club—a cooking and eating project we have been engaged in for several years. Now we want to spread the word, and to share recipes for the many meals we've enjoyed.

If you are already in the habit of cooking in quantity, expressly to share food with your friends and family, then the idea of doing so on a regular schedule will resonate. If you're used to cooking on a smaller scale, you might enjoy the wider net you can cast with food, when you know it will be enjoyed in other homes.

This is a cookbook, first and foremost, but it is also a guidebook for starting your own Soup Club: the logistics (there are just a few), the essential tools (ditto), and stories (to caution and inspire).

Caroline, Courtney, Julie & Tina

On Oct 4, 2011, 11:15 AM, Tina Carr wrote:

Hi Ladies,

It's soup weather . . . would you guys be into a weekly soup club? Julie and I talked it through a little yesterday and if you're all interested we'll make a schedule, agree on the terms, and eat soup!

Let me know,
Tina

On Oct 4, 2011, 11:20 AM, Caroline Laskow wrote:

I'm in!

From: Courtney Allison   October 4, 2011, 12:09 PM
To: Caroline Laskow
Cc: Tina Carr, Julie Peacock
Re: Soup Club

I'm Curious. Sounds fun.
Sent from my iPhone

From: Julie Peacock   Tuesday October 4, 2011,
Subject: Re: Soup Club   12:26 PM
To: "Caroline Laskow"; "Tina Carr"
Cc: "Courtney Allison"

Me, too!

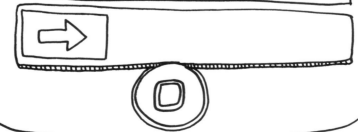

Tina

Courtney

Julie

Caroline

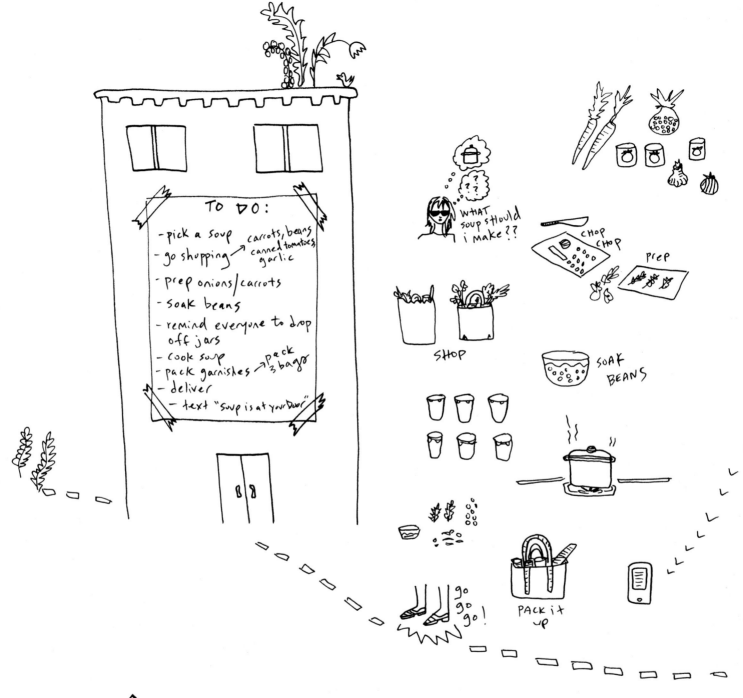

MY SOUP WEEK

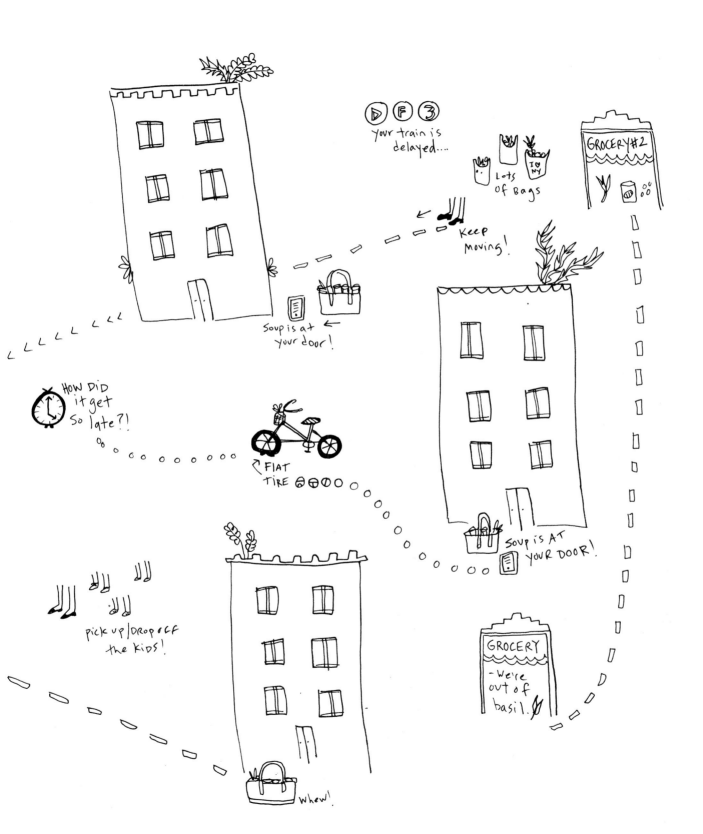

HOW TO BE A SOUP CLUB

GETTING STARTED

Previous cooking experience not required.
If you can boil water, you can make soup.

WHO IS IN SOUP CLUB? Anyone who likes soup and wants to play by the rules of Soup Club. Although there are no hard and fast rules for how many people can be in Soup Club, four members is a good start. Everyone's turn comes once a month, not too often or too infrequently.

The barrier to entry is low. More important than knife skills is a commitment to cooking at home on schedule and sharing the results. That means that your best friend—a wonderful cook—who has a job that takes her out of town for days at a time without notice might not be a great choice for Soup Club (but you can still share soup with her, because you're a food-sharing kind of person). On the other hand, do start a Soup Club with that intriguing co-worker whose homemade lunch always looks lovingly prepared, or your neighbor who waters your plants when you're away . . . and ask them to invite a couple of people they'd like to share food with, too.

WHEN DOES SOUP HAPPEN? Once a week. Establish your Soup Day and a time of day when the soup will be delivered so that you know which meal is covered. Wednesday by dinnertime works for us. You will start to plan around it, whether it's turning Soup Night into your family dinner or inviting friends over for a homemade meal (even if it wasn't cooked in your home).

HOW MUCH SOUP? One quart per adult is the basic rule of thumb. Depending on each member's household, this works out to four to eight quarts of soup each week, which even a small kitchen can handle. Most of these soups stand alone as a meal, and whether you live with other soup-eating mammals or not, you know you'll have some leftovers. Eight quarts is also great for dinner parties of eight to ten people.

WHERE DOES THE SOUP GET DELIVERED? Here's a key principle: THE COOK DELIVERS THE SOUP. Yes, once a month, the cook is doing ALL the work. Otherwise, everyone will get bogged down in a swamp of coordinating, and no one will be able to pick up soup at the same time. We have always left soup hanging on each other's doors. If your Soup Club shares a geographic point of convergence—work, house of worship, the gym, school—all the better.

Send word to your fellow Soup Club members to let them know what is awaiting them and how to eat it; texting was made for Soup Club notifications (see Roasted Winter Squash and Sweet Potato Soup, page 90).

AND to keep this well-oiled machine running, Soup Club recipients will drop off their CLEAN soup jars for next week's cook, usually no

N.B.: Your Soup Week will sometimes fall at the most inconvenient moment in your busy life. Just know that everyone's Soup Week will occur at an equally busy time for them. Get cooking.

SPEAKING OF RESTRICTIONS

Special Diets: One of our members is vegetarian, but she has not imposed that stricture on the rest of us, as her family is omnivorous. For the meat soups, it's usually okay to add meat on the side, or at the end of cooking, once you've set aside a portion for your resident vegetarian.

Allergies: One of our kids is allergic to fish, pistachios, and cashews. However, he doesn't react if he's not actually eating them, and his mom is comfortable serving those soups when he's not around.

In short, make sure your fellow soup club members know what you're all eating, or not eating.

A BIG STOCKPOT OF WATER takes 30 to 45 minutes to boil. You'll have time to take a shower.

later than the day before Soup Day. "Never return an empty jar," is a long-held principle in food-sharing communities, but in this case returning an empty jar breaks no social codes.

WHICH SOUPS?

Any kind of soup is fair game. For inspiration, you can:

    Consider **seasonality** (see Watermelon Gazpacho, page 114).

    Consider **your heritage and travels** (see Borscht, page 104).

    Consider **something new** (see Sunchoke Soup, page 89).

    Consider **restrictions** (see Turmeric and Greens, page 108).

BOTTOM LINE Giving soup is as satisfying as receiving soup. It's a virtuous cycle. Soup Club makes everyone happy.

You're Cooking a Lot of Soup

When cooking in this quantity, everything takes longer: chopping, sautéing, boiling, cooling soup for delivery. Also, you use more salt than you might think, and way more fridge space.

- All soup recipes in this book are written to yield eight quarts of soup. But it's really more like eight and a half to nine quarts of soup because we don't want you to be in the slightly heart-breaking position of not having enough soup to easily feed your friends, feed your family, and feed yourself (see Cuban Black Bean Soup, page 61).

- But maybe you're only cooking half of a lot of soup. All our recipes can be halved if you're looking to make a four-quart batch.

- Our recipes are written with the assumption that you are delivering soup to three other homes, and having soup yourself. Everything ultimately gets divided into four portions, including garnishes and sides.

- Bulking up a soup is possible, so add that leftover carrot, stray potato, or half onion, and taste as you go. As caretakers of orphaned produce we are inclusive. Soup is forgiving (see Roasted Parsnip Soup, page 85).

Essential Pantry and Basic Ingredients

Local, seasonal, and organic are the best choices for soup and for the planet. Humane and sustainable meats are ideal. But it's not always possible and that's okay. We'll still eat your soup, and you should, too.

Soup Club always uses these basic ingredients for cooking and serving our soups, and our recipes assume everyone's pantry is similarly stocked. Our list includes

- Kosher salt for cooking
- Eggs (always large)
- Butter (always unsalted)
- Dairy products (such as milk, yogurt, sour cream, and cream cheese), full-fat
- Extra-virgin olive oil
- Sea salt for finishing at the table

Feel free to substitute **LOWER-FAT DAIRY.** We always cook with full-fat, so your results may vary, but go for it.

- Black pepper
- Hard-to-deliver finishing oils (such as toasted sesame, walnut, or chili oil)
- Soy sauce

- Red pepper flakes
- Sriracha (or other hot sauce)
- Honey

ABOUT SALT When cooking large quantities of soup, salt in stages, tasting and adding salt as you go. We recommend using kosher salt, rather than table salt, in soup, because kosher salt lacks the additives and anti-caking agents that can give table salt a metallic taste. Also, because of its larger granules, you can more easily add a pinch. Sea salts and other finishing salts are great for sprinkling on top of a salad or other dish on which the salt won't dissolve.

There are tricks to undoing unfortunate episodes of oversalting. Among them, you can add sliced potato to the soup, simmer, then remove. Potatoes are salt sponges.

ABOUT BEANS Whenever possible, we cook dried beans from scratch to control the taste and texture, and to avoid added salt and preservatives. Give yourself two to twelve hours of lead time for the beans to soak.

If time is an issue, canned beans will work just fine (unless specifically noted in the recipe). When using canned, drain and rinse them well before putting them into your soup. Our recipes indicate how much liquid you might need to add in place of the bean cooking liquid reserved from dried beans.

With dried beans, there are two methods for soaking before cooking. Either way, start with sorting and rinsing them in a colander. Discard any shriveled or discolored beans.

- **Overnight soak:** Place the beans in a large bowl or pot, covered generously with cold water (by about three inches). Soak, covered, overnight or for eight to ten hours.

- **Quick soak:** Start with beans in a large pot, covered generously with cold water. Bring to a boil, turn off the heat, and cover. Let sit for one to two hours.

- **To cook soaked beans:** Drain, rinse, and place the beans in a large pot, covered generously with cold water. Bring to a boil, reduce the heat, and simmer, loosely covered, until well cooked, usually 30 to 60 minutes. Start to check after 25 minutes. Once the beans are tender enough to bite into, stir in a teaspoon of salt.

KNOW YOUR SPICES We are lucky to have a neighborhood spice market whose stock is incredibly fresh and intense. One tablespoon of their crushed red pepper flakes is very different from one tablespoon of the faded pizza parlor variety. Our recipes are written for the strong stuff, so you have to figure out the potency of your spices, then adjust.

MEET GHEE AND OTHER HELPFUL FATS For cooking, your primary oils should be regular olive oil and the "neutral" oils, like peanut or vegetable, that don't add flavor. But consider making room for some other helpful fats, including the following:

- **Ghee,** a shelf-stable clarified butter that is most common to Indian cooking, has a toasty-nutty-butter flavor thing going on. It also makes amazing popcorn (subbed for the popping oil), and can be found, jarred, in health food stores and Indian markets.

- **Coconut oil,** like ghee, is shelf-stable, has a delicate aroma, and gives a silky luxe coating to everything it touches, including dry skin and frizzy hair.

- **Schmaltz**—rendered chicken (or duck or goose) fat—is a revelation. Nothing burns, and food cooked in it tastes magically savory. Admittedly, saving up schmaltz from your roast chickens is

somewhat laborious, so if you can snag some from a fancy food shop, it's worth sticking in your freezer.

- **Finishing oils.** Then there are those last-minute, equally useful oils. These are simple, powerful flavor shortcuts, well worth the investment. Much like a pinch of crushed red pepper or freshly grated Parmigiano-Reggiano, a drizzle of appropriate oil enhances almost all soups, salads, stews, beans, dips, and spreads.

Tools for Cooking and Delivery

You don't need many tools for soup, but these are essential:

- **A very large stockpot.** Fourteen-quart capacity is recommended. You can't make eight quarts of soup in an eight-quart soup pot; you need room to work, stir, simmer, and blend.
- **An immersion blender** (also called a stick or hand blender). For any soups that need to be pureed, an immersion blender does the job, right in the same pot. Traditional blenders can't take the hot liquids. Allowing eight quarts of soup to cool completely can take a while. Then you have to transfer the pureed soup into yet another big soup pot, creating more dishes to wash.
- **A food processor.** Very helpful for making pestos and chopping anything (especially hard vegetables like carrots, parsnips, and onions) in large quantities.
- **A supply of tote bags.** Make sure your bags are sturdy! We like these flat-bottomed, somewhat wide and shallow canvas totes. We usually wrap the jars in a dish towel or newspaper for extra cushioning. Sometimes we borrow the universal takeout food technique and line the bottom of the bag with cardboard.
- **A supply of soup jars.** We use sturdy glass jars, because they're strong; they'll take your hot, hot soup; they're dishwasher-safe; and they don't retain flavors. A one-quart, wide-mouth jar is perfect for ladling, travel, storage, and even straight-from-the-jar eating if you're so inclined. And the tinier ones are just right for pesto and other garni.

IN HEAVY SOUP CLUB ROTATION are toasted sesame oil, hot chili oil, walnut oil, pumpkin seed oil, fancy olive oil, and a tiny vial of white truffle oil.

And Speaking of Delivery

- **Let the soup cool.** You can't deliver piping hot soup unless you have asbestos bags and hands. Ladle hot soup into jars for faster cooling, keeping lids off until jars are cool enough to touch.

- **Good soups can go bad.** Soup can't go unrefrigerated for hours on end. The rule of thumb is two hours off the heat (or out of the refrigerator). We err on the side of extra caution when delivering fish and meat soups, or on very hot days, when a personal handoff is highly recommended.

- **Good soups can be saved for another day.** Most soups freeze well, but those with dairy or coconut milk, not so much. They're edible, after thawing and reheating, but kind of unappetizing because the milk can separate.

Soup Up Your Soup in the Privacy of Your Own Home

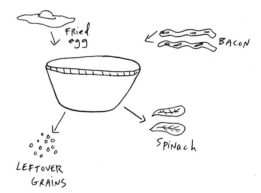

- Bacon makes everything better (unless you're a vegetarian). But really, all soups can be enhanced by the introduction of a well-placed protein. Roasted Asparagus Soup (page 84) with baked salmon? Classic. Senegalese Peanut Soup (page 101) with shredded chicken? Yes! Red Lentil Curry (page 57) over tofu? Hell yes!

- In fact, a bed of fresh greens is also a great way to go should you be feeling less carnivorous. Try lining your bowl with fresh spinach or kale and ladling piping hot soup on top. If you have leftover roasted veggies, put 'em in Roasted Parsnip Soup (page 85). Do it!

- How about Beck Chicken Chili (page 132) served over Cheddar Cornbread (page 183)? Yes, that's right, crumble the cornbread right into the bowl. Or add pasta, remembering that sometimes soup is a sauce. Then add bacon, because everything's better with bacon. Or, in a pinch, sausage.

BROTHS

Making broth is not rocket science. It's almost technique-free.
Water and a bunch of minimally prepped ingredients
simmered in a pot make broth. The process bears a suspicious
resemblance to making soup.

YOU MAY NOT THINK you're a homemade broth kind of person, but you'll never know until you try. Broth needs time on your stove, but that time is almost entirely unattended, so you can make broth spontaneously if you have onions, carrots, celery, and a couple of bay leaves. If you make (and freeze, see below) a big pot of broth every so often, you'll have it ready to go for soup. A broth should taste good on its own, so sample it after it's been cooking for a while, and add more salt or other seasonings as needed.

BROTH STARTERS   Keep a few zipper bags in your freezer for:

- Vegetable remainders (leek tops, half-used onions, mushroom stems, celery bulbs).
- Meat bones, chicken carcasses, a short rib that never got eaten.
- Parmesan rinds (they lend a special savory-saltiness when simmered).

STRAINING BROTH   Fish out the really big solids first, using tongs, a spider, or a slotted spoon. Then, line a colander with cheesecloth, and set it on top of your broth-storage pot or bowl. Set this in your sink and then carefully pour the broth from your gigantic stockpot.

STORING BROTH   Broth will keep for up to a week in the refrigerator and for several months in the freezer. Freeze broth in smallish containers for easy defrosting. You can reduce broth, making it more of a concentrate, by continuing to simmer it after you've strained out the solids, until the volume has gone down by about half. Then you can freeze the broth in ice cube trays (evict the cubes into a freezer bag once they are solid). Just add some boiling water to thaw.

WHAT IS STOCK AND WHAT IS BROTH?
You can really go down the rabbit hole on this one. There is a difference, having to do with salt (broth has it; stock doesn't) and the bone-to-meat ratio of your starting ingredients. Ultimately, however, the differences are more germane to restaurant kitchens and culinary schools. What we make and use, we call broth. We like our homemade versions, and we strongly encourage you to make your own, too. If you use store-bought, look for low-sodium broth, with a simple list of real food ingredients rather than added "flavors."

Some vegetables like **FENNEL, BEETS, AND CAULIFLOWER** can be too strong or turn bitter in your broth and in every future soup your broth creates, so be mindful of balance.

VEGETABLE BROTH

MAKES 8 QUARTS

To roast or not to roast the vegetables, that is the question—I have settled on a clear broth that requires a lot of fresh vegetables but involves no roasting or browning, and my reasoning is this: Cleanup is easy and the flavors are pronounced. Begin building your soup on this foundation with confidence. // TINA

- 1 head of **garlic** (10 to 12 **cloves**), smashed
- 3 medium **yellow onions**, quartered
- 12 **carrots**, roughly chopped
- 10 **celery stalks**, roughly chopped
- 2 **parsnips**, roughly chopped
- 2 large **leeks**, trimmed, cleaned (see Note), and roughly chopped
- 1 pound **mushrooms**, quartered
- 1 bunch **flat-leaf parsley**
- 6 to 8 sprigs **thyme**
- 5 **bay leaves**
- ¼ cup **peppercorns**
- ¼ cup **coriander seeds**
- 9 quarts cold **water**
- 1 tablespoon **salt**, plus more to taste

Put all the ingredients in the stockpot.

// Bring to a boil, reduce the heat, and simmer for 1½ hours, loosely covered. Taste and add more salt if needed.

// Allow the broth to cool, then strain and discard the vegetables.

NOTE: *Leeks are notoriously dirty. Split them lengthwise, spread the layers apart, and rinse vigorously in cold water before cutting.*

CHICKEN BROTH

MAKES 8 QUARTS

Every other week I have a ritual of making this broth. I freeze chicken carcasses or bones from the meals in between and then set a big pot on the stove to simmer for the afternoon. On my Soup Club week I often use a good portion of this as the base of my soup. Otherwise I freeze the broth in ice cube trays and save the cubes in zipper bags to use in cooking throughout the week. // COURTNEY

- 2 to 3 **chicken carcasses**, or 5 pounds assorted chicken parts, bone-in
- 6 **garlic cloves**
- 2 medium **yellow onions**, quartered
- 3 to 5 **carrots**, roughly chopped
- 3 **celery stalks**, roughly chopped
- 9 quarts cold **water**
- 1 tablespoon **salt**, plus more to taste

Put all the ingredients in the stockpot.

// Bring to a boil, reduce the heat, and simmer for 2 to 3 hours. Taste and add more salt if needed. Skim and discard the foam occasionally.

// Allow the broth to cool, then strain, and discard the vegetables and bones.

// Refrigerate for at least 8 hours. With a large shallow spoon, skim the fat from the broth, if desired. (This is schmaltz, and it's delicious to use for sautéing vegetables or other soup ingredients; see page 22.)

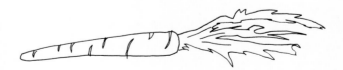

BEEF BROTH

MAKES 8 QUARTS

This broth is so rich on its own, it needs only a few additions to make full-bodied soup: noodles (as in the Faux Ramen, page 40), or lots and lots of leeks (see Leek Soup, page 106).

Prepare at least a day in advance, so it has time to chill. The marrow bones give off a lot of fat, which is easily removed once it solidifies. // CAROLINE

- 3 pounds **beef short ribs**, cut crosswise into 3-inch pieces (see Note)
- 2 pounds **beef marrow bones**, cut crosswise into 3-inch pieces
- 3 **carrots**, roughly chopped
- 4 **celery stalks**, roughly chopped
- 2 medium **yellow onions**, quartered
- 2 **bay leaves**
- 9 quarts cold **water**
- 1 tablespoon **salt**, plus more to taste
- 2 teaspoons freshly ground **black pepper**

Put all the ingredients in the stockpot.

// Bring to a boil, reduce the heat, and simmer for 3 to 4 hours, loosely covered. Skim and discard the foam occasionally. Taste and add more salt if needed.

// Fish out the short ribs and marrow bones. Using a chopstick (or similar skinny utensil), dig out any remaining marrow from the bones and stir it back in the pot. Allow the broth to cool, then strain and discard the vegetables.

// Refrigerate for at least 8 hours, then remove any fat that has solidified on top.

NOTE: *The short-rib meat can be pulled from the bones and reserved for Faux Ramen (page 40) or can be eaten, still warm from the pot, sprinkled with salt, as a guilty-pleasure Cook's Snack.*

FISH BROTH

MAKES 8 QUARTS

Talk to your local fishmonger about setting aside normally discarded bones and heads for you. However, do NOT use salmon, mackerel, or other oily fish, as they will add a lot of oil to the broth and impart an unpleasant flavor. // JULIE

- 6 pounds **fish bones** and **heads of non-oily fish** like halibut, cod, or flounder, gills removed, rinsed well
- 6 **garlic cloves**, smashed
- 2 medium **yellow onions**, quartered
- 6 **carrots**, roughly chopped
- 6 **celery stalks**, roughly chopped
- 2 cups **dry white wine**
- 8 sprigs **thyme**
- 8 sprigs **flat-leaf parsley**
- 2 **bay leaves**
- 1 tablespoon **whole peppercorns**
- 2 **whole star anise**
- 9 quarts cold **water**
- 1 tablespoon **salt**, plus more to taste

Put all the ingredients in the stockpot.

// Bring to a boil, reduce the heat, and simmer uncovered for 25 to 30 minutes. Skim and discard the foam occasionally. Taste and add more salt if needed.

// Strain the broth and discard the vegetables and fish bones. Let cool before storing.

SOUPS OF ASSEMBLY

Homemade broth is not required for every soup, but there is a category of recipes that allows you to show off the time you've spent on good simmering: the Soups of Assembly. The broth is the whole point, and that's where the majority of cooking happens. But there's still work to do: chopping, sorting, and bundling up ingredients for delivery, and including the assembly instructions. Each diner has the freedom to strike just the right balance of heat, salt, and umami at the table.

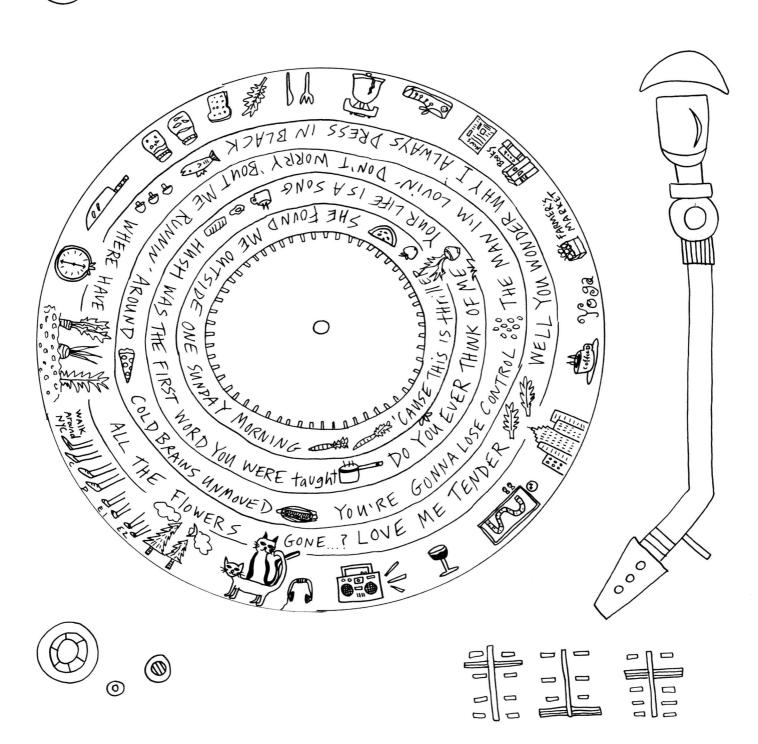

EGG DROP SOUP

MAKES 8 QUARTS

When I was a kid and stayed home sick from school, Egg Drop Soup was the cure-all meal my mom made for me. I still find myself making it whenever I'm under the weather, but I also make it for a simple weeknight dinner. Check that each Soup Club mate has four eggs for finishing at home. // COURTNEY

8 quarts **Chicken Broth** (page 30)

DIVIDED INTO 4 PORTIONS, FOR DELIVERY

8 **garlic cloves**, smashed

4 ounces **fresh ginger**, peeled and sliced into 1-inch pieces

16 **scallions**, thinly sliced

1 cup **cornstarch**

1 pound **extra-firm tofu**, drained and cut into ½-inch cubes

1 pound **ham**, cut into ½-inch cubes

1 pound **mushrooms**, thinly sliced

2 bunches **leafy Chinese greens** (like **bok choy**), thinly sliced

In a small bowl, whisk the cornstarch and ¼ cup broth to combine, then whisk the mixture into the soup.

// Crack 4 eggs into a small bowl and whisk thoroughly. Remove the soup from the heat and stir vigorously in one direction to create a vortex in the center of the swirling soup. Pour the egg mixture slowly in a steady stream into the soup while you continue stirring. Delicate ribbons will form.

// Serve with soy sauce, tofu, ham, mushrooms, scallops, and greens to add tableside.

FOR DELIVERY: Include 2 quarts broth and the packaged garlic, ginger, scallions, cornstarch, tofu, ham, mushrooms, and greens.

TO SERVE: Reheat the broth and bring to a boil. Add the garlic, ginger, and half the scallions. Reduce the heat and simmer, loosely covered, for 15 minutes. Use a spider to scoop the solids from the broth and discard.

FAUX PHO

MAKES 8 QUARTS

Traditional Vietnamese pho is redolent of beef, but we've invented a vegetarian version that pays respect to the Pho flavors with the addition of broiled ginger, which brings complexity and a caramel-like depth to the broth. // TINA

8 quarts **Vegetable Broth** (page 30)

4 ounces **fresh ginger**

16 **star anise**

16 **whole cloves**

8 **cinnamon sticks**

DIVIDED INTO 4 PORTIONS, FOR DELIVERY

1½ pounds **shiitake mushrooms**, brushed clean and thinly sliced (about 5 cups)

12 **garlic cloves**, thinly sliced

2 14-ounce packages **extra-firm tofu**, sliced into ½-inch cubes, or **Tofu Croutons** (page 43)

1 pound **rice noodles** (or a thin pasta, like angel hair), cooked

1 pound **bean sprouts**

16 **scallions**, thinly sliced

1 bunch Thai or regular **basil** and/or **cilantro**, chopped (about 1 cup)

1 small bunch **mint**, finely chopped (about ½ cup)

4 **limes** (or **lemons** as a substitute)

Peel the ginger and cut into 8 equal pieces. Broil the ginger on high for 10 to 15 minutes, flipping each piece when the edges of each side have browned. Remove from the broiler and allow to cool.

// Cut four 8-inch squares out of cheesecloth. In the center of each cloth place 4 star anise, 4 whole cloves, 2 cinnamon sticks, and 2 pieces of ginger. Gather the four corners of each cloth and secure the bundles with kitchen twine.

FOR DELIVERY: Include 2 quarts of broth, a spice bundle, and the packaged mushrooms, sliced garlic, cubed tofu (or Tofu Croutons), noodles, scallions, basil/cilantro, mint, and bean sprouts, plus 1 lime.

TO SERVE: Reheat the broth and bring to a boil. Add the mushrooms, sliced garlic, spice bundle, tofu, and 3 tablespoons soy sauce. Reduce the heat and simmer, loosely covered, for 30 minutes. Remove the spice bundle.

Heat the noodles and place in the bottom of each bowl. Pour in the broth. Top the soup with the bean sprouts, scallions, basil/cilantro, and mint. Squeeze some lime juice over the top and season with soy sauce, Sriracha, salt, and pepper.

FAUX RAMEN

MAKES 8 QUARTS

This Soup of Assembly welcomes your tasty leftovers. It is fully faux, and in the privacy of my own home, if there's good broth containing some kind of long pasta, kimchi, and an egg, that's enough. The version pictured has leftover Porchetta-esque Pork Butt (page 206), chili paste, Kimchi, and Kale Chips, plus quick-cooking rice noodles. Eat this out of a really big bowl, with room to assemble, admire, and eat the unique composition. Check that each Soup Club mate has one egg per person for finishing at home. // CAROLINE

> 8 quarts **Beef Broth** (page 31), **Chicken Broth** (page 30), or **Vegetable Broth** (page 30)
>
> **DIVIDED INTO 4 PORTIONS, FOR DELIVERY**
>
> 1 pound long **noodles**, cooked and tossed with a little **neutral oil** to keep from sticking
>
> 4 cups **protein**: cooked meat and/or tofu, diced (see Tofu Croutons, page 43)
>
> 4 cups **vegetables**, cut into bite-size pieces: cooked corn and mushrooms, bamboo shoots, bean sprouts, or any other vegetables you have lying around that are ready to be eaten
>
> 2 cups **Kimchi**, homemade (page 175) or store-bought
>
> **Kale Chips** (page 168) or roasted seaweed strips
>
> 12 **scallions**, chopped

Once the packages are assembled . . . your work is done. Next step, prepare **The Weekender** (page 201). Enjoy.

FOR DELIVERY: Include 2 quarts broth and the packaged noodles, protein, vegetables, kimchi, kale chips, and scallions.

TO SERVE: Reheat the broth, adding 2 teaspoons soy sauce. Ramen should be salty. Meanwhile, reheat the noodles, protein, and vegetables (a quick zap in a microwave is easiest). Fry the eggs just until the whites are set; the yolks should still be runny.

Put the cooked noodles, protein, and vegetables in the bottom of each bowl. Pour in the broth. Slide an egg on top of the broth. Add the kimchi, and tuck in the kale chips or seaweed. Sprinkle with scallions.

TOPPINGS

A good topping completes your soup.
It is the accessory that makes a meal work.

BASIC CROUTONS

MAKES 8 CUPS

Croutons add crunch and texture and are perfect on nearly any soup or salad. // JULIE

- 2 loaves **day-old bread**, cut into ½-inch slices and cubed
- 6 to 8 tablespoons **olive oil**, melted **butter**, or **flavored nut oil** such as walnut
- 2 **garlic cloves**, minced
- ¼ cup finely chopped **fresh herbs**, such as chives or oregano
- 2 teaspoons **smoked paprika** (optional)
- ¼ teaspoon **red pepper flakes** (optional)
- **Salt**
- Freshly ground **black pepper**

Preheat the oven to 400°F.

// Place the bread in a medium bowl and drizzle the cubes with the olive oil or butter. Sprinkle with the garlic, herbs, and paprika and red pepper flakes, if using. Salt and pepper to taste and mix well.

// Spread the seasoned bread cubes in a single layer on two rimmed baking sheets and bake for 12 to 15 minutes, stirring once, or until the bread just starts to turn golden around the edges. Let cool on the baking sheets. Store in an airtight container.

AMANDA'S GRILLED CHEESE CROUTONS

MAKES 32 CROUTONS, ENOUGH TO SERVE 8

Amanda Cohen, the chef-owner of Dirt Candy, the inventive "vegetable" restaurant in Manhattan, messed with perfection—the grilled cheese sandwich—and came up with the perfect crouton. // CAROLINE

- 8 slices **sandwich bread**
- 8 slices **melting cheese** (sharp cheddar and Gruyère are good choices)
- 2 to 3 tablespoons **butter**, softened

Melt a schmear of butter in a frying pan over medium heat. Assemble 4 cheese sandwiches—2 slices of cheese per sandwich—buttering the outside of the bread. Fry the sandwiches for 2 minutes on each side, weighed down (with a foil-wrapped brick or can of tomatoes on top of a plate).

// Take the sandwiches out of the pan and let them cool off for a few minutes, then cut each sandwich into 8 tiny triangles or cubes, as desired.

TOFU CROUTONS

MAKES ABOUT 4 CUPS

Khalil, our talented food stylist for this cookbook, shared with us his technique for tofu "croutons." // TINA

- 2 12- or 14-ounce packages **extra-firm tofu**, drained (see page 34)
- 4 tablespoons **olive oil**
- 1 teaspoon **salt**, plus more to taste

Lay the blocks of tofu between clean dish towels or a few layers of paper towels on a rimmed plate. Balance a cutting board weighed down with a heavy object (such as a can or two of tomatoes) on top of the tofu. Press the tofu for as little as 20 minutes at room temperature, or for as long as a day (in the refrigerator) if you plan ahead. After pressing, pour off the liquid and remove the towels. Cut the tofu blocks into ½-inch cubes.

// Preheat the oven to 425°F.

// Place the tofu cubes onto a large rimmed baking sheet and toss with the olive oil. Spread out in a single layer. Bake, stirring occasionally with a spatula, for about 25 minutes, or until golden brown.

// Transfer to a plate lined with a paper towel to drain, and sprinkle with salt immediately. Serve right away or keep refrigerated for up to a week.

PESTO

We like basil and pine nuts, of course, but we think pesto can be any combination of fresh herbs with olive oil, garlic, some nuts or seeds, cheese, lemon juice, and salt. It's a simple formula. We use our playful riffs on pesto frequently, both deliberately and spontaneously. Mustard green pesto brightens a bean soup like Chickpea, Roasted Squash, and Farro Soup (page 67). Kale-parsley pesto combined with Crème Fraîche (page 47) is a luscious finishing touch to pureed Roasted Asparagus Soup (page 84). Use all the fennel fronds left over from Tomato-Fennel-Chickpea Soup (page 110) for the Futurist pesto topper.

THE FORMULA

8 cups **fresh herbs** and/or greens (1 to 2 large bunches herbs and your choice of greens like kale, arugula, mustard greens, dandelion greens), loosely packed, to fill the bowl of a food processor

Freshly squeezed **lemon juice** (start with 1 lemon)

1 teaspoon **salt**, or to taste

Our Favorite Combinations

Classic Basil and pine nuts

Neoclassic Basil, some parsley, and pepitas (raw green pumpkin seeds)

Modern Kale and parsley, walnuts

Futurist Fennel fronds, some parsley, walnuts, and pepitas

Alternative Arugula, mint, and pine nuts

Tricolore Basil, pine nuts, and fresh tomatoes

Midcentury Modern Dill and almond

Lower East Side Mustard greens, chives, and pecans

What the *%*^ is Lovage Lovage, parsley, basil, and pepitas

Autumnal Thyme, beet greens, and pepitas

1 **garlic clove**

½ cup **grated cheese**, a combination of **Parmigiano-Reggiano** and **Pecorino** or straight Parmigiano-Reggiano

½ to 1 cup **nuts**, lightly toasted (or not; go rogue)

½ cup **olive oil**, plus more as needed

Put the herbs/greens, lemon juice, salt, garlic, cheese, and nuts in a food processor. Pulse the processor a few times to get everything a little mashed down, then run the processor and drizzle in the oil, starting with about ½ cup. Stop, scrape down the sides with a spatula, and taste. Salt? Check. Lemon juice? Check. Consistency? Check.

PARSLEY-DILL GREMOLATA

Gremolata is pesto's lactose-intolerant cousin. This bright, simple condiment is made of finely chopped herbs, mixed with lemon and garlic and traditionally served with meat and seafood dishes. A gremolata can be intense and sometimes bitter on its own; a little goes a long way. It's great with chilled Potato Leek Soup (page 73) or Sunchoke Soup (page 89). // TINA

1 cup fresh **flat-leaf parsley**, leaves finely minced (stems reserved for Vegetable Broth, page 30)

½ cup fresh **dill**, leaves finely minced

1 **garlic clove**, finely minced

Finely grated **zest** of 2 small **lemons**

Salt

Mix the minced parsley and dill with the garlic and lemon zest until well blended. Salt to taste and refrigerate in an airtight container. It's best when used within a couple of days.

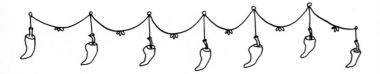

CHILI OIL

MAKES 2 CUPS

Having homemade chili oil on hand is wonderful when you want to add some heat to soups, pastas, or greens. Use one part fresh chile peppers to four parts oil (you can use one part red pepper flakes to 8 parts oil to save time). If using fresh, choose Red Savina habanero for a lot of heat, long slim cayenne peppers for medium heat, or jalapeños or serranos for less heat. Try drizzling over the Chickpea, Roasted Squash, and Farro Soup (page 67) or Lentil Squash Salad (page 162). // JULIE

- 2 cups **neutral oil**, such as sunflower (or light olive oil)
- ½ cup chopped fresh **chile peppers** (pith and seeds removed for less heat) or 1 tablespoon **red pepper flakes**
- 4 **garlic cloves**, smashed (optional)

Heat the oil in a small pan and add the chiles and the garlic, if using. Simmer for 5 minutes, then remove from heat and let cool to room temperature. Remove the garlic cloves and pour the chili oil into a glass container with a tight-fitting lid. Store at room temperature for up to 2 weeks.

HERBED QUESO FRESCO

MAKES ABOUT 1 POUND

Queso fresco is a firm-textured white cheese that is slightly salty and mildly tangy. It is a welcome addition to soups, salads, grilled vegetables, and so much more, especially when mixed with fresh herbs. This version is delicious with Beck Chicken Chili (page 112), Corn and Red Pepper Salad (page 159), and Winter Corn Chowder (page 93). // JULIE

- 1 14-ounce package **queso fresco**
- 1 cup loosely packed chopped fresh **cilantro** (or other herbs, such as mint, parsley, chives, or thyme)

Crumble the queso fresco into the bowl and toss thoroughly with the cilantro.

CHEESE CRISPS

MAKES 36 CRISPS

This is the best single-ingredient garnish ever. I specify the cheese here because the flavor of a good imported Parm matters. Grate the cheese yourself because packaged grated cheese has anti-clumping additives that interfere with melting. // COURTNEY

- 6 ounces **Parmigiano-Reggiano cheese**, grated (about 2½ cups)

Preheat the oven to 350°F.

// Line two rimmed baking sheets with parchment paper. Make mounds using approximately 1 tablespoon of grated cheese spaced 2 to 3 inches apart. You should be able to get a dozen mounds per sheet.

// Bake 6 to 8 minutes, until the cheese melts, spreads, bubbles, and turns golden brown. Rotate and switch the pans once halfway through cooking. These are best enjoyed within a day. Store them at room temperature on a plate tightly covered with plastic wrap.

CRÈME FRAÎCHE

MAKES 2 CUPS

Crème fraîche has a consistency similar to yogurt or sour cream, but is less tangy. You can cook with it and it freezes well. Each batch will taste a little different depending on the flavor of the dairy products used and the time it sits unrefrigerated. Buttermilk is used here, while some other recipes call for yogurt. Either way, make sure "active cultures" are listed on the label. You will be rewarded with heavenly batches if you let two simple ingredients do their thing on your counter. // TINA

> 3 tablespoons cultured **buttermilk** (with active cultures)
>
> 2 cups **heavy cream** (see Note)

Combine the buttermilk and cream in a nonreactive bowl (such as ceramic or glass) and whisk gently to combine. Loosely cover the bowl with plastic wrap and leave unattended at room temperature for 8 to 24 hours. This range depends on the dairy products you start with and the temperature of your room.

// Some bubbling may occur almost immediately, which is a sign that the bacteria in the buttermilk are at work. This acid in the mixture prevents spoiling while it is unrefrigerated on your counter. Crème fraîche will keep for about 10 days in the refrigerator, where it will continue to thicken.

NOTE: *Look for buttermilk and heavy cream without additives, and begin with the least pasteurized cream you can find. Ultra-pasteurized still works but will take closer to 24 hours to thicken.*

Crème Fraîche Is Magical

In a time before Soup Club, Caroline casually shared some wisdom with me one day at the playground: "Crème fraîche makes everything taste like food, and it's more socially acceptable than just adding butter to everything." I was grateful for the tip, since I had leftover pasta in need of a makeover before landing on my dinner table in forty minutes. Avoid the rather expensive store-bought small tubs and make your own.

HARISSA

OREGANO

Enhanced Crème Fraîche

These variations start with one cup of crème fraîche. The additions get mixed in by hand. Salt and pepper all to taste.

Herbed 3 tablespoons mixed minced fresh herbs (such as sage, thyme, marjoram, chives, tarragon, parsley) and 2 teaspoons finely grated lemon zest

Curried Beet 4 tablespoons roasted and pureed beet and 1 tablespoon curry powder

Horseradish Beet 4 tablespoons roasted and pureed beet and 1 tablespoon horseradish

Chipotle-Adobo 1 to 2 tablespoons canned adobo sauce and a finely minced chipotle pepper for extra heat. (The sauce will thin the crème fraîche.)

Harissa 1 to 2 teaspoons

CHIVE

CHIPOTLE ADOBO

LEMON ZEST

DILL

CURRIED BEET

TRY PESTO

Nuts and Seeds

Toast your nuts. Some cooks skip this step to save time, but you'll really miss out if you do. Toasted nuts and seeds are deeper in flavor and crisper in texture, and they make the perfect accompaniment to soups and salads. They can also stand alone as an easy snack or appetizer (see pages 234–235).

THERE ARE A FEW WAYS TO TOAST NUTS AND SEEDS:

In a dry pan over medium heat for a few minutes. Stir frequently.

On a rimmed baking sheet in your oven at 325°F for 10 to 15 minutes. Stir halfway through.

On a rimmed baking sheet in your toaster oven on medium for 3 to 5 minutes. Stir halfway through.

However you do it, as soon as the nuts and seeds become fragrant, they're done, and they should be removed from the pan immediately. Be careful not to burn them. They go from toasty-delicious to charred and inedible very quickly.

Store toasted nuts and seeds for up to a week in an airtight container at room temperature or in the freezer for several months.

PEPITAS

PECANS

BRAZIL NUTS

CASHEWS

PINE NUTS

WALNUTS

ALMONDS

PEANUTS

HAZELNUTS

PISTACHIOS

SUNFLOWER SEEDS

CHILI-LIME PEPITAS

MAKES 2 CUPS

I made these specifically to top chilled Avocado-Arugula Soup (page 115), but they work with all the gazpacho variations (pages 114–120). // CAROLINE

- 2 teaspoons **olive oil**
- 2 cups (about ½ pound) **pepitas** (raw green pumpkin seeds)
- 1 teaspoon **chili powder**
- ¼ cup freshly squeezed **lime juice** (from about 2 limes)
- ½ teaspoon **salt**

Heat the oil over medium heat in a large frying pan, and add the pepitas. When the pepitas start to color and "pop," add the chili powder, lime juice, and salt. Stir well to coat. Remove from the heat after 3 to 5 minutes, when the lime juice has evaporated completely.

Cool in the pan before packing up. May be made a day in advance. Store, in a jar or container with a tight-fitting lid, at room temperature.

// PART TWO //

ALL THE SOUPS

It feels like there should be a drumroll intro here, but soup is a more easygoing kind of player. We've organized these recipes according to how Soup Club evolved, moving through all the vegetarian soups into our later fish- and meat-based options. Each of us has well-loved recipes—Tina's Green Split Pea Soup (page 57), Julie's Roasted Parsnip Soup (page 85), Caroline's Filipino Healing Soup (page 128), and Courtney's Beef Mole Chili (page 140)—and there has been much experimenting along the way. It's remarkable how many places canned tomatoes and coconut milk can take you, from Senegal to Thailand to Spain and back home again.

BEANS

A pot of cooked beans is almost soup, just in need of some flavorful liquid and maybe a few helpful vegetables for texture. Soup Club started with several weeks of different beans and legumes, and we all come back to beans regularly. Dried or canned, beans are easy to keep on hand; they are substantial, vegetarian (but taste so good with some meaty enhancement), and inexpensive. Extra cooked beans become salads and dips, and they freeze perfectly (drain them first, then seal in a zipper bag). But enough with the infomercial, and on to the soups.

I was all set to follow Caroline in the Soup Club rotation we'd just set up, and I'd done some thinking: Red lentils and curry were the two ingredients my debut soup had to have. Seeing Caroline on the playground the day before her soup was scheduled to appear on my doorstep, I excitedly leaked my plan. Caroline, surprised, replied, "That's so strange . . . I'm making a red lentil curry."

Did I get that right? The sounds and shrieks of playing children confused my hearing. I remember showing up on the first day of eighth grade, wearing exactly the same shirt as my best friend and looking like a total dork. Caroline's soup plan was the adult version of that tween nightmare.

I decided to debut with a tried-and-true Green Split Pea, and to remember that Soup Club is not a competitive sport. // TINA

GREEN SPLIT PEA SOUP

MAKES 8 QUARTS

Heat the oil in the stockpot and add the onions. Sauté until soft, about 7 minutes. Add the garlic, celery seeds, and cumin seeds and sauté for 2 more minutes, until fragrant.

// Add the potatoes, parsnips, and split peas. Cover with the vegetable broth or cold water and add the bay leaves and thyme.

// If using, add half of a chipotle pepper and a spoonful of the adobo sauce. Add more later, if desired.

// Bring the soup to a boil, skim and discard the foam as necessary, and reduce to a simmer. Depending on the age of the peas, the cook time can vary wildly. Begin checking for doneness after 45 minutes. Continue cooking until the peas are soft; this may take up to 2 hours. Stir occasionally, to avoid scorching.

// Remove and discard the bundle of thyme and the bay leaves. Using an immersion blender, puree the soup to desired consistency. (I like some texture in mine.) Add the salt and additional water to thin if necessary. Season with pepper to taste and more salt if needed.

¼ cup **olive oil**

3 medium **yellow onions**, chopped

1 head of **garlic** (about 10 cloves), minced

1 tablespoon **celery seeds**

2 tablespoons **cumin** seeds

3½ pounds waxy **potatoes,** such as Yukon Gold, scrubbed and chopped into ½-inch cubes (about 10 medium potatoes)

1 pound **parsnips**, peeled and chopped into ½-inch cubes

3 pounds (about 6½ cups) dried green **split peas**, picked through and rinsed well

5 quarts **vegetable broth** or cold water plus more to thin as needed

5 **bay leaves**

8 sprigs **thyme,** tied together with kitchen twine

1 canned **chipotle pepper in adobo sauce** plus 2 teaspoons adobo sauce (optional)

2 tablespoons **salt**, plus more to taste

Freshly ground **black pepper**

Basic Croutons (page 43), made with smoked paprika

2 cups **Enhanced Crème Fraîche** (page 48), made with chipotle and adobo

1 bunch **flat-leaf parsley**

FOR DELIVERY

Include one quarter of the crème fraîche, croutons, and parsley.

TO SERVE

Reheat the soup and thin with water as needed. Top with a dollop of crème fraîche, a handful of croutons, and a scattering of parsley leaves.

CAROLINE: I was shocked, *shocked* when I realized the tumult Tina had internalized over my unknowingly ruining her soup debut. Rest assured, dear reader, that we have worked through our complicated emotions and love each other's legumes, without rancor.

I am not historically a joiner of clubs, but I said yes to Soup Club because Courtney, Julie, and Tina already felt like my tribe. Being my mother's daughter, I can't help but cook in quantity, and I welcomed having a purpose for it at least once a month.

So with my joiner's zeal, I volunteered to take the first week. This was more out of blind faith than because I had a concrete plan or recipe. I wanted to use the CSA haul taking up precious kitchen real estate: potatoes, sweet and regular; loads of onions and garlic; a random head of green cabbage; and way too many carrots. Cumin always works with orange, rooty produce, and I knew I had fresh ginger, plus coconut milk and a jar of ghee (a helpful fat; see page 22), in my pantry. An on-the-spot curry came together, given heft by the quick-cooking red lentils and quinoa I had overlooked for too long. This soup is open to further interpretation—winter squash or parsnips would work well in place of the carrots and sweet potatoes; cooked chickpeas could substitute for lentils—establishing the first rule of Soup Club: improvisers always welcome.

// CAROLINE

RED LENTIL CURRY

MAKES 8 QUARTS

Heat the oil in the stockpot. Add the celery, onion, garlic, and ginger and sauté until soft, about 7 minutes. Add the cumin, curry paste, salt, and red pepper flakes. Continue to cook until the spices are aromatic, about 5 minutes.

// Add the ghee, stir to help it melt, then add the carrots, cabbage, potatoes, and lentils. Continue to cook for 10 minutes, stirring occasionally.

// Add the coconut milk and 2 quarts of cold water. The liquid should just cover everything, so add more water if needed. Bring to a boil, reduce the heat, and simmer, loosely covered, for 20 minutes.

// Meanwhile, prepare the quinoa: Bring 4 cups lightly salted water to a boil, add the quinoa, reduce the heat, cover, and simmer for 15 minutes. Remove from the heat, fluff with a fork, and let the quinoa sit, covered, until it's time to add it to the soup.

// Check the lentils, carrots, and potatoes for doneness. If they're not soft, continue cooking and check every 5 minutes. Then take off the heat, and puree with an immersion blender. Add the cooked quinoa, and stir well. Season with salt and pepper.

3 tablespoons **neutral oil**

6 **celery stalks**, roughly chopped

4 medium **yellow onions**, roughly chopped

10 **garlic cloves**, smashed

8 ounces fresh **ginger**, peeled and thinly sliced

2 teaspoons freshly ground **cumin** (pulverize whole cumin seed in a coffee grinder just before using for the most potent flavor)

2 tablespoons **red Thai curry paste**, or to taste

2 tablespoons **salt**, plus more to taste

1 tablespoon **red pepper flakes**

¼ cup **ghee**, **coconut oil**, or **butter**

2 pounds **carrots**, roughly chopped

½ medium head **cabbage**, finely sliced (or shredded in a food processor)

3 **sweet potatoes**, skin on, cut into eighths

3 **baking potatoes**, skin on, cut into eighths

1 pound **red lentils**

3 13.5-ounce cans unsweetened **coconut milk**, well stirred

2 cups **quinoa**, rinsed thoroughly (or buy prerinsed)

Freshly ground **black pepper**

4 packages **naan**, **pappadam** (crispy, Indian bean-flour wafers), or **pita**

1 large bunch **cilantro**

FOR DELIVERY

Include a package of the naan, pappadam, or pita and one quarter of the cilantro.

TO SERVE

Reheat the soup. Top with cilantro leaves, and use the bread for dunking.

CSA stands for Community Supported Agriculture. CSA members pay upfront for a share of an entire season of produce from a regional farmer. This early bulk payment enables a farmer to plan for the season, purchase new seed, make equipment repairs, and more. Weekly or biweekly, from June until October or November, your farmer will deliver that share of produce to a convenient drop-off location in your neighborhood (adapted from JustFood.org).

GS
Turnip
1/4

68
1/4

My first soup (night and day)

// COURTNEY

11:00 p.m.

I need to be up at 5:30 a.m. I'm standing in front of my stove and all four burners are covered with my four largest pots set to boil. Front burners: my first attempt at vegetable broth since college. Back burners: beans.

11:15 p.m.

The broth has simmered long enough. The beans are soft. They should be. Yes, that means I didn't start to make this soup until nearly 8 p.m. Yes, I did know last week that I needed 8 quarts of soup for tomorrow.

11:30 p.m.

The entire apartment fills with the smell of onions, garlic, jalapeño, carrots, and green pepper. It's delicious and somehow energizes me. Everything is coming together and suddenly I have faith in this soup. I like it. I think it is going to be good. I can do this. I can be a good spouse, feed and clothe and instill good values in my kids, have a fulfilling professional career, and have hobbies. I am awesome. I add the beans. I set the stove to its lowest setting.

12:00 a.m.

I go to bed. How in the world did it get to be midnight?!

5:15 a.m.

The alarm goes off. It is dark. I head to the kitchen and gingerly take the lid off the pot. I grab the immersion blender from the drawer. Steam rises from the pot. Is there anything worse than the smell of garlic at 5:30 in the morning? I open the window.

5:40 a.m.

I'm done. The soup is perfect—not too thin, not too thick. I line up containers and begin to fill. After the fourth quart I know I have a problem. I need six full quarts to deliver and enough soup for dinner for my own family. The sixth quart is only three-quarters full. I dip a quarter cup out of the other five containers. There isn't enough to feed my family tonight. I pack the six quarts with toppings in three bags, one for Caroline, one for Julie, one for Tina. I slip the containers into the fridge and vow to tell no one.

6:10 a.m.

The house stirs. My husband is up. The kids follow. I can't do this. Who am I to think I can work full time, be a good spouse, feed and clothe and instill good values in my kids, have a fulfilling professional career, and have hobbies? I am insane.

5:15 p.m.

After work I race home and get the soup out of the fridge. I dash back out the door to make deliveries. An hour or so later my phone buzzes. "Wow this is great!" "Wonderful soup . . . thank you . . . and the toppings . . . impressive." "Thanks! It's a big hit with Dan and the boys." I remember why I'm doing Soup Club. I pick up the Thai takeout menu and breathe deeply. No soup for us tonight, but I can totally do this. Crazy, but worth it for sure.

CUBAN BLACK BEAN SOUP

MAKES 8 QUARTS (I PROMISE)

4 tablespoons **neutral oil**

5 medium **yellow onions**, roughly chopped

5 medium **carrots**, diced

4 **celery stalks**, diced

6 **garlic cloves**, minced

3 medium **jalapeño peppers**, seeded and minced

3 tablespoons ground **cumin**

3 tablespoons **chili powder**

1 tablespoon **salt**, plus more to taste

9 cups cooked **black beans**, from 1½ pounds dried

5 quarts **vegetable broth**

3 28-ounce cans chopped **tomatoes**, with their juice

3 **bay leaves**

Freshly ground **black pepper**

2 cups **queso fresco**

1 bunch **cilantro**

1 16-ounce bag **tortilla chips**

Heat the oil in the stockpot. Add the onions, carrots, and celery and sauté until soft. Add the garlic and jalapeño and sauté for another minute, taking care not to burn the garlic. Add the cumin, chili powder, and salt. Continue to cook until the spices are aromatic, about 5 minutes.

// Add 6 cups of the beans, the vegetable broth, the chopped tomatoes, and bay leaves to the pot and bring to a boil. Reduce to a simmer and cook, loosely covered, for at least 2 hours, stirring occasionally.

// When the beans are beginning to fall apart, remove the pot from the heat and discard the bay leaves. Blend the soup with an immersion blender until smooth. Stir in the reserved beans. Season with salt and pepper.

FOR DELIVERY

Include one quarter of the queso fresco, cilantro, and tortilla chips.

TO SERVE

Reheat the soup, ladle into bowls, and crumble in a portion of queso fresco. Top with cilantro leaves and tortilla chips.

" **JULIE:** My husband and I have been in search of the perfect black bean soup since sharing a bowl at a favorite café in a Long Island beach town one winter. This one fits the bill. Thanks, Courtney. P.S. Add avocado.

2 pounds dried **chickpeas**, soaked (see About Beans, page 21) or 14 cups cooked or canned (drained and rinsed)

6 pints **cherry** or **grape tomatoes**, halved

½ cup **olive oil**

6 teaspoons **salt**, plus more to taste

2 heads **garlic** (about 20 cloves), coarsely chopped

2 teaspoons **saffon threads**

1 tablespoon ground **cumin**

2 teaspoons **sweet paprika**

3 medium **yellow onions**, finely chopped

4 bunches **spinach** or about 40 ounces, stemmed and rinsed well (or bagged baby spinach), divided

Freshly ground **black pepper**

½ pound **Manchego cheese**

Crostini (page 179) made with garlic

A wave of excitement rolled over me; I was next up in Soup Club rotation. With the anticipation, though, came a tiny bit of trepidation. Even though we'd been known to share food—some granola here, a quiche there—being in Soup Club required a new level of commitment. I needed inspiration.

After dropping off my two older kids at school, I rode over to the farmer's market with my youngest daughter, Sabine, loaded in the back of my bucket bike. The spinach caught my eye right away. Bright and tender, with a little farm grit still clinging to it, the spinach reminded me of living and eating in Spain. I bought several bunches and plenty of garlic and onions and headed for home, stopping off for pricey, but essential, saffron. It was time to marry a favorite combo of mine, spinach and chickpeas, into a happy soup union.

When I was twenty-five, I moved to Madrid to study Spanish and was eager to explore Spanish food, even though I was a vegetarian at the time and Spain is a meat-loving country. Thankfully, I fell in with Uta, the adorable, vibrant German girl sitting next to me in Spanish class. And a vegetarian! We bonded immediately, exploring tapas bars and restaurants in pursuit of *vegetariano* food, *"sin jamón, por favor?"* We quickly realized that Spain does vegetables well. One of my very favorites was the tapa called Espinacas con Garbanzos, Spinach with Chickpeas. Popular in southern Spain, its origins are North African. It's made with cumin and garlic and generous amounts of olive oil, and it's best with crostini or fresh baguette. Inspired by that dish, and in honor of my friendship with Uta still strong nearly fifteen years later, this soup was born. // JULIE

SPANISH CHICKPEA AND SPINACH SOUP

MAKES 8 QUARTS

Preheat the oven to 450°F.

// Drain and rinse the soaked chickpeas and add them to the stockpot. (If using canned, go to the next step.) Cover them generously with 5 to 6 quarts of cold water and simmer, loosely covered, until al dente, 45 to 60 minutes. Drain using a colander over a large bowl, reserving the cooking liquid.

// Meanwhile, place the tomatoes cut side up on two foil-lined rimmed baking sheets. Drizzle with ¼ cup of the olive oil and sprinkle with 2 teaspoons of the salt. Roast for 25 to 30 minutes, until the tomatoes begin to dehydrate and caramelize. Remove from the oven and set aside.

// Using the flat side of a large knife on a cutting board or using a mortar and pestle, mash the garlic to a paste with the saffron threads and 2 teaspoons of the salt.

// Ladle out 3 cups of the chickpea cooking liquid into a small bowl. If using canned chickpeas, use 3 cups water. Add the garlic-saffron mash, cumin, and paprika to the bowl of liquid. Stir together and set aside.

// In the stockpot, heat the remaining ¼ cup of olive oil and sauté the onions until soft, about 7 minutes.

// Add the garlic-spice liquid to the stockpot and simmer for a couple minutes more.

// Add the chickpeas, 3½ quarts reserved chickpea cooking liquid, roasted tomatoes, and the remaining 2 teaspoons of salt and bring to a boil. (If you are using canned chickpeas, add 3½ quarts water.) Reduce the heat and simmer for 15 more minutes.

// Add 3 bunches of the spinach in stages. Stir each bunch through, and cover the pot briefly to wilt the leaves. Remove from the heat.

// Thin with additional chickpea liquid or water if the soup is too thick. Season with salt and pepper.

If you're going for a **SPANISH-INSPIRED MEAL**, serve with Potato Tortilla (page 228) and Almonds with Rosemary (page 235). Otherwise, roasted vegetables (see page 169) or Escarole, Grapefruit, and Hazelnut Salad (page 156) work well, too.

FOR DELIVERY
Include one quarter of the remaining spinach, the cheese, and the crostini.

TO SERVE
Reheat the soup and ladle into bowls lined with spinach leaves. Grate cheese over the top and serve with crostini.

Lentils are fast-cooking legumes, so if you've prepped your ingredients, you can make and serve (or pack up) this soup within about an hour. One snowy evening, my friend James (a woman) made a big pot of this soup for both of our families of five, and the ten of us were well fed and happy.

James's slightly tart, umami* rich soup was the perfect antidote to a winter that had been growing long and cold. Since it turned out to be right up the narrow culinary alley of Oscar, my middle child, it has become a staple for me. He is a picky eater and has a singular allegiance to mac and cheese, but he quickly gobbled up a giant portion before racing back to his construction project. // TINA

LENTIL SOUP

MAKES 8 QUARTS

Heat the oil in the stockpot. Add the onions, carrots, and celery. Sprinkle with the salt and sauté the vegetables until they begin to soften, about 7 minutes. Add the garlic and cumin and sauté for another couple of minutes, until the mixture is aromatic, taking care not to burn the cumin.

// Add the lentils, thyme, bay leaves, pepper, and vegetable broth. Bring the soup to a boil, reduce the heat, and simmer, loosely covered, for about 20 minutes, or until the lentils are tender. Skim off and discard any foam that rises to the top.

// Remove the soup from the heat and discard the 4 bay leaves. Add the tamari or soy sauce. Using an immersion blender, lightly puree the soup. This adds a creamy texture to the soup, but still leaves most of the lentils intact. Season with salt and pepper.

¼ cup **olive oil**

3 medium **yellow onions**, finely chopped

8 medium **carrots**, finely chopped

5 **celery stalks**, finely chopped

1 tablespoon **salt**, plus more to taste

6 to 8 **garlic cloves**, minced

1 tablespoon ground **cumin**

3½ pounds brown or green **lentils** (about 8 cups), rinsed and drained

8 sprigs **thyme**, leaves only

4 **bay leaves**

1 teaspoon freshly ground black **pepper**, plus more to taste

6 quarts **vegetable broth**

¼ cup **tamari** or **soy sauce**

4 **lemons**

4 ounces **Parmigiano-Reggiano** or **Pecorino Romano** cheese

FOR DELIVERY
Include 1 whole lemon and one quarter of the cheese.

TO SERVE
Per James's instructions: "Squeeze some lemon juice into each serving bowl before adding the heated soup, and rub more juice on the rim for those who sip out of the bowl." Grate some cheese over each bowl.

The term umami *was coined by professor Kikunae Ikeda in 1908 to describe the fifth primary taste sensation (the other four being salty, sweet, sour, and bitter). The common translation from Japanese is "pleasantly savory." Think soy sauce, ketchup, and Parmigiano-Reggiano cheese.*

This soup, adapted from the cookbook *Zuppe*, by Mona Talbott, is complex, mellow, and sweet. The bursts of orange butternut squash contrast beautifully with the earthy shades of the chickpeas and farro, livened up with a tableside drizzle of chili oil. Using dried chickpeas here is key, because the base of the soup is their cooking liquid. If you're new to farro, it's a nutty, chewy, low-gluten ancient grain and can be found in most supermarkets near the grains or bulk/dried goods. Serve with some Marinated Brussels Sprouts (page 171).
// JULIE

CHICKPEA, ROASTED SQUASH, AND FARRO SOUP

MAKES 8 QUARTS

¾ cup **olive oil**, divided

4 medium **yellow onions**, finely chopped

10 **carrots**, finely chopped

10 **celery stalks**, finely chopped

5 teaspoons **salt**, plus more to taste

2 heads **garlic** (about 20 cloves), peeled and divided

7 to 9 sprigs **rosemary**, leaves only, finely chopped

1 pound dried **chickpeas**, soaked and drained (see About Beans, page 21)

4 pounds **butternut squash**, peeled and chopped into 1-inch cubes

2 cups **farro** (13 ounces), rinsed and drained

2 large bunches **Red Russian kale** or other greens, chopped

Freshly ground **black pepper**

4 ounces **Pecorino** cheese

1 cup **Chili Oil** (page 46)

Preheat the oven to 400°F.

// Heat ¼ cup of the olive oil in the stockpot and add the onions, carrots, and celery. Sprinkle with 2 teaspoons of the salt and sauté the vegetables until they begin to soften, about 7 minutes. Mince half of the garlic and stir in along with the rosemary. Sauté for another few minutes.

// Add the chickpeas and 4 quarts water and bring to a boil. Reduce the heat and simmer, covered, for 45 to 60 minutes, or until the chickpeas are tender. Skim away any foam that comes to the surface.

// Meanwhile, spread the remaining garlic cloves and butternut squash cubes out in a single layer on two foil-lined rimmed baking sheets. Drizzle each pan with 2 tablespoons of the oil and sprinkle with 1 teaspoon of the salt. Toss with your hands to evenly coat. Roast for 20 to 25 minutes, until tender and browned.

// While the chickpeas are simmering and the squash is roasting, bring 3 quarts water to a boil and add the farro. Boil for about 20 minutes, or until al dente. Drain the farro over a medium bowl and reserve the cooking liquid.

// Meanwhile, heat the remaining ¼ cup of olive oil in a large skillet and add the chopped kale and the remaining teaspoon of salt. Sauté until wilted, about 5 minutes, and set aside for delivery.

// Add the roasted squash and garlic and cooked farro to the chickpeas and simmer for about 20 more minutes. If the soup seems too thick, thin with the reserved farro cooking liquid. Season with salt and pepper.

FOR DELIVERY

Include one quarter of the sautéed kale, cheese, and chili oil.

TO SERVE

Reheat the soup and the kale separately. Lay some of the kale in the bottom of each soup bowl and ladle the soup over it. Grate cheese on top and drizzle with chili oil.

5 jalapeño peppers

4 dried **ancho chile peppers**

Salt

5 tablespoons **olive oil**

2 tablespoons **cider vinegar**

3 medium **yellow onions**, diced

1 head of **garlic** (about 10 cloves), minced

2 pounds **carrots**, cut diagonally into thick ovals (Bradley's tip, for a more rustic texture)

¼ cup **tomato paste**

3 tablespoons ground **cumin**

2 tablespoons ground **coriander**

6 large **bell peppers**, preferably in 3 different colors (red, orange, yellow), cored, seeded, and diced

1 12-ounce bottle **lager** or **IPA**

2 pounds **dried beans**: a mix of kidney beans, black beans, and navy or cannellini beans, soaked (see About Beans, page 21); or 15 cups assorted cooked/canned beans, drained and rinsed

3 28-ounce cans diced **tomatoes**, with their juice

6 sprigs **thyme**

3 **bay leaves**

2 tablespoons **Marmite** or **Vegemite**

⅔ cup unsweetened natural **peanut butter**, preferably salted

¼ cup boiling **water**

Freshly ground **black pepper**

2 cups **sour cream**

12 **scallions**, finely chopped

1 bunch **cilantro**, chopped

1 16-ounce bag **tortilla chips**, or **Cheddar Cornbread** (page 183) or **Corn Casserole** (page 187)

Ian, my husband, learned to cook when he was in law school. He worked like a dog to get through those three years, with studying and brief mental breaks scheduled out to the minute. To sustain himself, he chose a short list of recipes to master. Though Ian will be the first person to announce that he disapproves of a meat-free diet, this veggie chili is one of his best meals. Ian's guiding principle is simply to load up the pan with some of his favorite vegetables and beans—three colors of each, that's a rule—then add just enough liquid to make it spoon-worthy. This version benefits from the habits of two committed vegetarians: my cousin Mike, who was born in England and adds Marmite or peanut butter to almost every soup he makes (I opted for both); and our friend Bradley, whose chili secret is to add a bottle of beer. // CAROLINE

THE DUDES' CHILI

MAKES 8 QUARTS

Preheat the oven to 325°F.

// Roast the jalapeños and anchos on a rimmed baking sheet for 15 minutes, then let cool. In a food processor, puree the peppers with a large pinch of salt, 1 tablespoon of the olive oil, and 1 tablespoon of the vinegar. Add more salt, oil, and vinegar if needed, for flavor and consistency. Set this chili paste aside. (May be made up to 1 week in advance.)

// Heat the remaining olive oil in the stockpot. Add the onions, garlic, carrots, tomato paste, cumin, coriander, a tablespoon of salt, and 1 tablespoon of the chili paste. Stir to combine, and sauté for 10 minutes. Add the bell peppers and beer and cook for 10 more minutes.

// Drain and rinse the beans, then add them to the stockpot. Add the two cans of tomatoes, fill the two empty cans with cold water, and add the water to the pot. Bundle the thyme and bay leaves in a piece of cheesecloth, tie it up with kitchen twine, and add to the pot. Simmer, loosely covered, for 40 minutes, or until the beans are soft. (If starting with cooked beans, add them after the tomatoes have simmered for 30 minutes.)

Potatoes and leeks are modest headliners, but when they are cooked just so with cream and herbs, a star is born. If, that is, the ingredients are fantastic. I learned this the hard way one week when I was shopping and cooking for Soup Club away from home.

I found myself at an out-of-town grocery store examining a sad-looking and solitary bundle of leeks, dripping from its recent run-in with the produce section's sprinkler. It made no sense to proceed with my soup plan, but I stayed the course. In the end—as expected—the leeks were far outnumbered by the potatoes, which were too starchy. To make matters worse, I didn't calculate the proportions correctly. The result was a really thick potato mash. I called it soup, but that was a stretch.

The lesson I learned is this: Keep an open mind when you do your shopping. Know what's in season and delicious and available where you are; and most of all, when the recipe calls for just a couple ingredients, make sure that they are top notch. If they're not, have the confidence to experiment with substitutions or change direction with a new recipe. // TINA

POTATO LEEK SOUP

MAKES 8 QUARTS

Melt the butter in the stockpot over medium-low heat and add the white and pale green leeks, the salt, and the pepper. Cook, stirring frequently to prevent browning, for 12 to 15 minutes, or until the leeks are translucent and soft. Add the potatoes and the leek green stock or vegetable broth.

// Meanwhile, prepare the herbs. Cut away the dill stems from the leaves. Mince the leaves and tie the stems with kitchen twine. Bundle the tarragon and the star anise in a square of cheesecloth bound with twine. Add all of these herbs to the stockpot.

// After the soup has come to a boil, reduce the heat and simmer for 20 minutes, or until the potatoes are soft. Remove the dill stems and the star anise–tarragon bundle.

// Remove the soup from the heat. Using an immersion blender, puree to desired consistency. Mix in the cream and season with salt and pepper.

½ cup (1 stick) **butter**

6 to 7 pounds **leeks** (12 to 14 large leeks), trimmed and cleaned, pale green and white parts cut into ¼-inch rounds, dark green parts reserved

¼ cup **salt**, plus more to taste

1 teaspoon freshly ground **black pepper**, plus more to taste

5½ pounds creamer or **fingerling potatoes**, scrubbed and halved (I like to leave the potato skins on for texture in the finished soup)

5 quarts **leek green stock** (see below) or **vegetable broth**

1 bunch **dill**

1 bunch **tarragon**

4 **star anise**

1 pint **heavy cream**

4 **demi-baguettes**

Dill Butter (page 71)

4 whole **nutmegs**, for grating (optional)

FOR DELIVERY

Include a demi-baguette, ¼ cup of the dill butter, and 1 whole nutmeg to grate on top, if desired.

TO SERVE

Gently reheat the soup. If using the nutmeg, grate tableside. Serve a slice of demi-baguette slathered with dill butter alongside.

LEEK GREEN STOCK: Cut the dark green leek stems into 3-inch lengths and bring to a boil in 6 quarts cold water. Reduce the heat and simmer for an hour. Strain and discard the leek greens. Make up to 2 days ahead.

10 bunches **asparagus**, woody ends removed, cut into 2-inch pieces (about 10 pounds)

3 pounds **leeks** (about 6 large **leeks**), trimmed and cleaned, white and light green parts chopped

½ cup **olive oil**

1 tablespoon **salt**, plus more to taste

Freshly ground **black pepper**

6 quarts **vegetable broth** or **chicken broth**

2 cups **Crème Fraîche** (page 47)

Parsley-Dill Gremolata (page 44)

4 **lemons**

The first time I made this soup I was longing for spring on a dreary February day and impulsively bought all the asparagus I could find. The asparagus was delicious even though it was out of season, but that craving hit me in the pocketbook. I recommend making this soup when asparagus is readily available, abundant, and affordable; or rename it Million Dollar Soup and give your club mates a taste of spring in midwinter. // COURTNEY

ROASTED ASPARAGUS SOUP

MAKES 8 QUARTS

Preheat the oven to 350°F.

// Arrange the asparagus and leeks in a single layer on two or three foil-lined rimmed baking sheets. Drizzle with the oil and toss the vegetables with your hands to evenly coat. Sprinkle with 1 tablespoon salt and 6 to 8 hearty grinds of black pepper. You may need to roast in batches depending on the size of your oven.

// Roast the vegetables for 20 to 30 minutes, until the asparagus pieces are wilted and the leeks are beginning to brown, rotating the location of the sheets in the oven halfway through cooking. Remove the sheets from the oven.

// Add all of the leeks and asparagus to the stockpot and add the broth. Bring to a boil, reduce the heat, and simmer. Remove the soup from the heat. Using an immersion blender, puree the soup until smooth. Season to taste with salt and pepper.

FOR DELIVERY
Include one quarter of the crème fraîche and gremolata plus 1 lemon for zesting on top of the soup.

TO SERVE
Reheat and serve topped with crème fraîche, gremolata, lemon zest, and freshly ground black pepper.

A few years ago, my late-December birthday coincided with a massive blizzard that snowed in New York City. Caroline had given me a cookbook by Les Dames d'Escoffier, and I read it while the snow created a blanket of quiet over the city, discovering a roasted parsnip soup that seemed to fit the weather perfectly. I was amazed at how this pale, nubby tuber related to the popular and bright carrot could overcome its "roots" and become a somewhat sophisticated crowd-pleaser.

Look for parsnips that are firm, have smooth skin, and are medium in size. The larger ones are often flavorless and they may have cores that need to be cut out and discarded. On the other hand, the smaller ones are often immature and, after being peeled, are not much bigger than a matchstick. Tap into your inner Goldilocks and find ones that are just right. // JULIE

ROASTED PARSNIP SOUP

MAKES 8 QUARTS

Preheat the oven to 425°F.

// Spread the parsnips in a single layer on two foil-lined rimmed baking sheets. Drizzle with the oil and toss with your hands to evenly coat. Sprinkle with 2 teaspoons of the salt. Roast for 30 to 40 minutes, until tender and golden.

// Meanwhile, melt the butter in the stockpot over medium heat. Add the shallots, garlic, and remaining 4 teaspoons salt and sauté until shiny, stirring occasionally, about 3 minutes. Add the celery and carrots and cook until soft, about 10 minutes. Add the white wine, broth, roasted parsnips, and beans and bring to a boil. Reduce the heat and simmer, loosely covered, for 15 to 20 more minutes.

// Stir in the cream and cayenne pepper. Remove the soup from the heat and, using an immersion blender, puree the soup. Season with salt and black pepper

FOR DELIVERY	TO SERVE
Include one quarter of the crostini, chive-studded chèvre, chives, and walnuts.	Reheat the soup and finish with chopped chives before eating. Slather the crostini with chive-studded chèvre and press with toasted walnuts. Serve alongside the soup.

9 pounds **parsnips**, peeled and roughly chopped

½ cup **olive oil**

2 tablespoons **salt**, plus more to taste

4 tablespoons (½ stick) **butter**

4 medium **shallots**, minced (about 2 cups)

6 **garlic cloves**, minced

8 **celery stalks**, roughly chopped

1 pound **carrots**, roughly chopped

2 cups dry **white wine**

4½ quarts **vegetable broth** or **chicken broth**

2 15.5-ounce cans **white beans** (Great Northern or cannellini), drained and rinsed (3 cups)

1 cup **heavy cream**

½ teaspoon **cayenne pepper**

Freshly ground **black pepper**

Crostini (page 179) with **Chive-Studded Chèvre** (page 179)

2 bunches fresh **chives**

2 cups chopped **walnuts**, lightly toasted

I ADDED WHITE BEANS to this soup the first time I made it because it ended up being way too thin after I pureed it. Because they impart a nice creaminess to the soup, I kept them in the recipe. You can also add a few cooked and peeled potatoes until the desired consistency is achieved.

3 tablespoons **vegetable oil**

¼ to ½ cup **Thai green curry paste**

6 quarts **vegetable broth** or **chicken broth**

6 16-ounce bags frozen **green peas**, thawed (take them out of the freezer about an hour before cooking)

2 16-ounce packages frozen **spinach**, chopped or whole leaf, thawed (see above)

14 **scallions**, divided

2 tablespoons **salt**, plus more to taste

2½ cups **Crème Fraîche** (page 47)

Freshly ground **black pepper**

1 bunch **mint**, leaves thinly sliced

Tofu Croutons (page 43) or 8 cups plain cooked **rice**

Sesame oil, toasted or spicy

LOOK
IN
HERE !
←

This freezer soup is a marriage of two of Nigella Lawson's delicious sweet pea recipes: the scallion-infused Slime Soup from *Feast* (which I've now read so many times the pages are falling out) and the green-curry–spiced Thai Scented Pea Puree from *Kitchen* (which is on its way to a similar fate). I like them both so much that I combined them into one pot of soup, adding frozen spinach for more flavor and color. As an added bonus, this is a quick low-skill-and-effort production—no peeling or chopping, just opening some packages. You can serve it hot or chilled. // CAROLINE

CURRIED GREEN PEA AND SPINACH SOUP

MAKES 8 QUARTS

In the stockpot, gently heat the oil (it shouldn't be too hot or the curry will scorch) and add the green curry paste. Stir it around the bottom of the pot.

// Add the broth, stir to distribute the curry, and bring to a boil. Add the peas, spinach, 6 whole scallions, and 1 tablespoon of the salt. Return to a boil, reduce the heat, and simmer, loosely covered, for 10 minutes.

// Check to make sure the peas are cooked through, then remove from the heat and fish out the scallions. Add ½ cup of the crème fraîche and puree with an immersion blender until smooth. Season with salt and pepper.

FOR DELIVERY
Include one quarter of the remaining crème fraîche and scallions, one quarter of the mint, and one quarter of the tofu croutons or rice.

TO SERVE
Reheat the soup and top each bowl with a dollop of crème fraîche, some chopped scallions, a sprinkling of mint, and some croutons. Drizzle with sesame oil. (If using rice instead of croutons, add a scoop to each bowl before ladling in the soup.)

My sister, Sara, and I lived together in Minneapolis just after we had graduated from college, and paging through cookbooks and trying new recipes was one of our favorite activities. Sara spent much of her free time exploring the farmer's markets and the large network of local food co-ops, and she was inspired to make beautiful meals for us. This soup was part of her repertoire, and the sweet, earthy aroma of toasted mustard and cumin seeds, key ingredients in this soup, would welcome me home. We hosted Thanksgiving that year in our cozy one-bedroom apartment, sharing this rich soup with our parents and some neighbors—a treasured memory.

You can substitute any variety of winter squash for the pumpkins or try mixing in sweet potatoes. To finish, consider adding Kale Chips (page 168) or stirring in a spoonful of pesto made with thyme, parsley, and pepitas to add color and to balance the sweetness of the pumpkins. (Or see the pesto ideas on page 44.) // JULIE

SPICED PUMPKIN SOUP

MAKES 8 QUARTS

¼ cup **olive oil**

3 tablespoons **cumin seeds**

3 tablespoons **mustard seeds**

4 medium **yellow onions**, roughly chopped

3 tablespoons chopped peeled fresh **ginger**

2 teaspoons ground **cinnamon**

5 teaspoons **salt**, plus more to taste

4 small **pumpkins** (6 to 8 inches in diameter) or 10 pounds (about 34 cups) peeled and roughly chopped pumpkin

1½ pounds **carrots**, roughly chopped

1½ cups **powdered milk**

Freshly ground **black pepper**

4 **demi-baguettes**

2 cups **Crème Fraîche** (page 47)

2 cups **pepitas** (raw green pumpkin seeds), toasted

1 bunch **thyme**

Heat the oil in the stockpot over medium heat and add the cumin and mustard seeds. Toast the seeds until fragrant and lightly browned, being careful not to burn them, 3 to 4 minutes. Add the onions, ginger, cinnamon, and salt and sauté until the onions are soft, about 7 minutes.

// Put the chopped pumpkin and carrots in the stockpot with 3 quarts of cold water and bring to a boil. Reduce the heat and simmer, loosely covered, until the vegetables are tender, 20 to 30 minutes.

// Remove the soup from the heat. Stir in the powdered milk, and puree with an immersion blender. Add water if needed for the desired consistency. Season with salt and pepper.

PEELING PUMPKINS is easier than you might think: After washing the pumpkins thoroughly, dry them well and place on a cutting board. You want to place a kitchen towel under the pumpkin that you're about to slice to hold it in place. Turn the pumpkin on its side and slice ½ inch off each end. Grasping the pumpkin firmly, use a knife or a Y-shaped vegetable peeler to remove the skin. Cut the pumpkin in half, scoop out the seeds, and roughly chop.

FOR DELIVERY
Include 1 demi-baguette and one quarter of the crème fraîche, pepitas, and thyme.

TO SERVE
Reheat the soup and serve with a swirl of crème fraîche, a small handful of toasted pepitas, fresh thyme leaves, and chunks of warmed baguette.

Sunchokes, also known as Jerusalem artichokes, are homely, knobby root vegetables that take patience and, in my opinion, a lot of yogic breathing to thoroughly peel. I adored their nutty, sweet flavor but always felt intimidated by what I thought was their demanding preparation: I assumed you HAD to peel them. Then, one day, while paging through one of Deborah Madison's cookbooks, I learned that it wasn't necessary to peel sunchokes. Just scrub them well, and they're ready to go. Serve with Butter Lettuce and Radish Salad (page 156) or Spicy Roasted Broccoli (see page 170). // JULIE

SUNCHOKE SOUP

MAKES 8 QUARTS

Heat the oil in the stockpot and add the onions, garlic, celery, and 1 tablespoon of the salt. Sauté until the vegetables are soft, about 7 minutes. Add the potatoes and sunchokes and cook for another 10 minutes, or until they are lightly golden. Add the broth and the bay leaves and bring to a boil. Reduce the heat, cover, and simmer until the sunchokes and potatoes are tender, about 40 minutes.

// Remove the soup from the heat, discard the bay leaves, and stir in the remaining salt. Puree the soup with an immersion blender until smooth. Stir in the cream and add more broth if the soup needs thinning. Season with salt and pepper.

4 tablespoons **olive oil**

3 medium **yellow onions**, roughly chopped

8 **garlic cloves**, minced

6 **celery stalks**, roughly chopped

3 tablespoons **salt**, plus more to taste

3 pounds **red creamer potatoes**, scrubbed and quartered

6 pounds **sunchokes**, thoroughly scrubbed and roughly chopped

3 quarts **vegetable broth** or **chicken broth**, plus more if needed

8 **bay leaves**

1 cup **heavy cream**

Freshly ground **black pepper**

Basic Croutons (page 43), made with walnut oil

2 cups chopped **pistachios**, toasted and salted

Kale Chips (page 168)

Walnut oil (check that your Soup Club mates have their own supply at home)

FOR DELIVERY

Include one quarter of the croutons, pistachios, and kale chips.

TO SERVE

Reheat the soup and top with a handful of croutons, a spoonful of pistachios, a couple leaves of kale chips crunched on top, and a drizzle of walnut oil.

3 large **sweet potatoes** (about 3 pounds), scrubbed

2 **acorn squash** (about 2¼ pounds), halved and seeded

3 medium **butternut squash** (about 6 pounds), halved and seeded

⅓ cup **olive oil**

2 tablespoons **salt**, plus more to taste

½ teaspoon freshly ground **black pepper**, plus more to taste

1 bunch **mixed fresh herbs**, such as sage, rosemary, and thyme

1 head of **garlic** (about 10 cloves), peeled

4 tablespoons (½ stick) **butter**

2 medium **yellow onions**, chopped

8 to 10 **sage leaves**, thinly sliced

4 quarts **vegetable broth**

4 **cinnamon** sticks

1 teaspoon ground **cloves**

⅓ cup pure **maple syrup** (optional)

2 cups **Enhanced Crème Fraîche** made with fresh herbs (page 48)

1 bunch **chives**

FOR DELIVERY

Include ½ cup of crème fraîche and one quarter of the chives.

TO SERVE

Reheat and top with a dollop of crème fraîche and a sprinkling of chopped chives.

You can also **THIN THIS SOUP** with apple cider to add sweetness.

The following recipe calls for acorn and butternut squash, but any hard winter squash can be used. // TINA

ROASTED WINTER SQUASH AND SWEET POTATO SOUP

MAKES 8 QUARTS

Preheat the oven to 400°F.

// Wrap the sweet potatoes in foil and bake for about 1 hour, or until a fork slides easily into the flesh.

// Meanwhile, prepare the squash. Arrange the halved squash on two foil-lined rimmed baking sheets, with the cavities facing up. Evenly drizzle the oil over the squash and sprinkle with 1 tablespoon of the salt and the pepper. Distribute the fresh herbs and garlic cloves in the squash cavities and turn them over so that the skin side is facing up, stuffing in any herbs that are peeking out from under the squash.

// Bake the squash in the oven with the sweet potatoes for 30 to 60 minutes, or until the flesh is soft. (This cook time ranges widely, given that squash can vary in size and moisture.) As with the sweet potatoes, test their doneness by piercing the skin with a knife or the tines of a fork.

// Remove the squash and sweet potatoes from the oven and cool until they can be handled. Remove the herbs and scoop out the flesh of the squash, setting aside the garlic cloves. Unwrap and peel the sweet potatoes.

// Melt the butter in the stockpot, add the onions and the remaining salt, and cook for 8 to 10 minutes, until soft. Add the sliced sage, the roasted sweet potatoes, squash, garlic, broth, cinnamon sticks, and ground cloves. Mince and add in the roasted herbs as desired. Bring the soup to a boil, reduce the heat, and simmer for 30 minutes, loosely covered. Remove the soup from the heat and discard the cinnamon sticks. Puree the soup with an immersion blender until smooth.

// If the soup is too thick, thin with a little water. Taste and add the maple syrup if desired. Season with salt and pepper.

To: Courtney, Julie, and Caroline; From: Tina

This week's soup and stuff is a celebration of squash. It's everywhere this month! I finally roasted up the acorn squash that I had lying around. I added to that some herbs, a couple butternut squash, as well as that crazy-looking pumpkin creature that we got yesterday. (Anyone remember what it is called?) This morning I made sense of it all. It will be at your doorstep by 5. Enjoy!

To: Tina, Courtney, and Julie; From: Caroline

That's a Kuri squash. Yum.

HEARTY

We were trying to think of a commonality among all these soups, and couldn't. They are all over the map and the grocery store. Some, like the Summer Squash Soup or Winter Minestrone, are seasonally dependent, but others, like the Sun-Dried Tomato Soup, can be sourced from the inner aisles. Hearty soups defy easy categorization, but they will take the errant carrot, extra potato, strong spices, and big bunches of herbs. They're substantial and easily stand alone as meals. Get out your cutting boards.

This was created for a dead-of-winter Soup Club rotation. If you've hoarded corncobs in the freezer (see Summer Corn Hash, page 201, and Corn and Red Pepper Salad, page 159), your soup will be rewarded with a corn-stock base, a gift from last summer. The unadorned chowder is a canvas for all sorts of toppings, and I went a little crazy on that first delivery, including pickled jalapeños, cotija cheese, avocado, cilantro, sour cream, tortilla chips, and crumbled bacon. A Soup Club record (because sometimes Soup Club IS a competitive sport), but I've since refined the list. // CAROLINE

WINTER CORN CHOWDER

MAKES 8 QUARTS

Heat the butter and oil together in the stockpot and sauté the parsnips, leeks, onion, carrots, celery, and thyme until very soft, about 15 minutes.

// Add 2 pounds of the corn, all the edamame, the salt, and a generous grind of pepper. Cook for another 5 minutes, then add the corn stock. Bring to a boil and whisk in the masa harina paste. Reduce the heat and simmer, loosely covered, for 10 minutes.

// Remove the soup from the heat and briefly puree with an immersion blender, 5 to 10 seconds. You won't get a smooth soup, but breaking down some of the vegetables gives a creamier texture. Add the remaining pound of corn and simmer for 10 minutes. Season with salt and pepper.

// While the soup is simmering, char the jalapeños under the broiler for 5 to 10 minutes, and set aside. When they are cool enough to touch, chop them up, discarding the seeds if you want less heat.

5 tablespoons **butter**

1 tablespoon **olive oil**

2 pounds **parsnips**, peeled and diced (diced new potatoes can substitute for all or part of the parsnips)

3 large **leeks**, trimmed, cleaned, and finely chopped

1 large **red onion**, diced

4 **carrots**, diced

4 **celery stalks**, diced

3 tablespoons **thyme** leaves

3 pounds frozen **corn** (thawed on the counter about an hour before cooking)

1 pound frozen shelled **edamame** (thawed on the counter about an hour before cooking)

1 tablespoon **salt**, plus more to taste

Freshly ground **black pepper**

4 quarts **corn stock** (see below), **vegetable broth**, **chicken broth**, or **water**

⅓ cup **masa harina**, mixed with a little broth or water to form a thick paste (or finely ground cornmeal, if you can't find masa)

8 **jalapeño peppers**

12 slices cooked **bacon** (optional)

8 ounces **extra-sharp cheddar**, or ricotta salata

1 16-ounce bag **tortilla chips** or 4 **demi-baguettes**

———————

CORN STOCK: Put 10 to 14 corncobs in a large stockpot and cover with at least 6 quarts cold water. Bring to a boil, reduce the heat, and simmer for 1 hour. Discard the cobs. Refrigerate for up to a week or freeze for several months.

FOR DELIVERY	**TO SERVE**
Include one quarter of the jalapeños, bacon, cheese, and chips or baguettes.	Crumble the bacon into the soup before reheating. Top with the jalapeños and crumbled cheese. Serve the chips or warm baguette on the side.

¼ cup **olive oil**

2 medium **yellow onions**, chopped

8 **garlic cloves**, minced

3 bunches **mixed greens** (Swiss chard, mustard greens, and/or kale), finely chopped with stalk ends trimmed (about 15 cups)

1 tablespoon **salt**, plus more to taste

3 15.5-ounce cans **cannellini beans**, drained and rinsed

3 28-ounce cans diced **tomatoes**, with their juice

3 quarts **vegetable broth** or **chicken broth**, plus more if needed

8 inches **Parmesan rinds**

1 pound **carrots**, diced

1 medium **butternut squash**, about 3 pounds, peeled, seeded, and diced

3 medium **zucchini**, diced

3 medium yellow **summer squash**, diced

Freshly ground **black pepper**

4 **demi-baguettes**

2 cups chopped **fresh herbs** (flat-leaf parsley and oregano or whatever is in season and easy to find)

2 cups **Pesto** (page 44) made with kale and parsley

½ pound **Parmigiano-Reggiano** or **Romano cheese**

GRAB PARMESAN RINDS from your broth starter bag in the freezer (see page 29), or ask if your grocery store will give you some. If they sell their own grated cheese in the deli section, chances are they've got cheese rinds to spare.

This is a sort of "clean-out-the-fridge" soup, as any variety of vegetables will do. The soup's rich flavor comes from tossing your old Parmesan rinds into the soup as it cooks, so DO NOT skip this step! Also, the addition of the garlicky pesto brightens the soup and even gives it a little kick. If you don't have time to make the pesto, toss in the fresh herbs at the end and swirl in a touch of garlic paste (see Salads and Dressings, page 150). All three of my kids willingly shove big spoonfuls of this seasonal soup into their mouths. Truly, the highest of compliments. Pair this soup with Amanda's Grilled Cheese Croutons (page 43) and Winter Caesar Salad (page 158). // JULIE

WINTER MINESTRONE

MAKES 8 QUARTS

Heat the oil in the stockpot and add the onions, garlic, and mixed greens. Sprinkle with the salt and sauté until the vegetables are slightly wilted, about 10 minutes.

// Add the beans, tomatoes, broth, Parmesan rinds, carrots, and butternut squash and bring to a boil. Reduce the heat and simmer for 10 to 15 minutes, until the vegetables are tender but still firm.

// Add the zucchini and yellow squash and cook, loosely covered, for 10 minutes, or until all vegetables are tender. If the soup is too thick, add more broth or water.

// Before ladling the soup into jars, fish out and discard the gooey cheese rinds. Season with salt and pepper.

FOR DELIVERY	**TO SERVE**
Include 1 demi-baguette and one quarter of the herbs, pesto, and cheese.	Reheat the soup and stir in a few pinches of the fresh herbs. Add a dollop of pesto and grate cheese over the top. Serve with warm baguette.

CAROLINE: Julie's beautiful minestrone is the fancy first cousin of the Italian peasant *Ribollita* soup I love to make. Ribollita uses mostly just greens and beans, and old bread cubes (or croutons or crostini) get simmered into the soup at the end. But Julie's squash cubes elevate this still-rustic comfort soup, giving sweet balance to the greens.

6 cups raw **cashews** (about 2 pounds)

2 ounces dried **porcini mushrooms**

1 quart boiling **water**

¼ cup **olive oil**

2 **sweet onions** (such as Vidalia), quartered and thinly sliced

3 **celery stalks**, finely sliced

2 big bunches **flat-leaf parsley**, divided

2 tablespoons **salt**, plus more to taste

1 teaspoon freshly ground **black pepper**, plus more to taste

2 pounds **white button** or **baby bella mushrooms**, cleaned and roughly chopped

4 pounds **assorted mushrooms**, such as chanterelles, shiitakes, portobellos, oysters, or morels, cleaned

Large loaf of crusty **wheat bread**

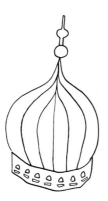

Portobello, baby bella, chanterelles, oysters, morels, shiitake, puffballs, porcini, and button . . . the sight and smell of the earthy fungi piled high on my counter takes me back to Russia, where I lived for three years after studying Soviet politics and Russian in college. Vodka, caviar, and borscht are considered to be archetypal in Russian culture, but gathering mushrooms deserves a spot on this list. It is to Russian families what apple picking is to their American counterparts.

I call for making your own cashew cream since store-bought versions often start with dry-roasted cashews and contain oil or other additives. The cashews need to soak for at least eight hours before pureeing, so plan ahead. Serve this mellow soup with Red Cabbage Salad (page 161). // TINA

MUSHROOM AND CASHEW CREAM SOUP

MAKES 8 QUARTS

Place the cashews in a large bowl and pour water over to cover by 2 inches. Set aside to soak at room temperature for 8 to 12 hours.

// When you are ready to make the soup, put the porcini mushrooms in a small heat-proof bowl and cover with the boiling water. Soak for 20 to 30 minutes.

// Meanwhile, heat the oil in the stockpot. Add the onions and celery and sauté until soft, about 7 minutes. Finely chop the leaves and top stems from one bunch of parsley and add them to the pot after the onions and celery have softened. Stir in the salt and pepper.

// While the vegetables are sautéing, pulse the button mushrooms in an upright blender with 5 cups cold water until roughly blended. You may need to do this in batches. Add these mushrooms to the stockpot and cook uncovered over medium-low heat for 10 to 15 minutes. The mushrooms will release a lot of liquid. Allow the liquid to reduce by about half. Rinse out the blender and set it aside (you will be using it again shortly).

// Chop the remaining cleaned assorted mushrooms.

// Rub the porcinis to loosen any grit and use a slotted spoon to remove them from the hot water they have been soaking in; they will have doubled in size. Finely chop the porcinis and strain the porcini soaking liquid through a square of cheesecloth (or coffee filter) and reserve.

// Stir all of the mushrooms into the stockpot. Pour in the strained porcini soaking liquid plus 1 quart cold water. Bring the soup to a boil, reduce the heat, and let it simmer for 15 to 20 minutes, until the mushrooms are cooked through and tender.

// Meanwhile, drain the water from the cashews and replace it with 6 cups cold, fresh water. Blend the cashews and water in an upright blender, in batches as needed, to achieve a very finely blended cream. While the soup is simmering, add the cashew cream and mix in by hand. Season with salt and pepper.

FOR DELIVERY

Include one quarter of the remaining parsley and the bread.

TO SERVE

Reheat the soup, taking care to ensure the cashew cream is well incorporated. Top with parsley leaves and serve with bread.

¼ cup **olive oil**

3 medium **yellow onions**, chopped

16 **carrots** (2 pounds), diced

1 head of **garlic** (about 10 cloves), minced

2 cups **sun-dried tomatoes** or 1 batch **Oven-Dried Tomatoes** (page 177), julienned

4 28-ounce cans diced **tomatoes**, with their juice

4 quarts **vegetable broth**

2 2-ounce bunches **basil**, leaves chopped

1 tablespoon **salt**, plus more to taste

1 teaspoon freshly ground **black pepper**, plus more to taste

8 **scallions** (white and green parts), sliced into rounds

Amanda's Grilled Cheese Croutons (page 43)

There's nothing like creamy tomato soup with a grilled cheese sandwich. But sometimes you want more tang and less cream. For those occasions, this soup hits the spot. Try lining your bowl with Spinach Polenta (page 199) and ladle the soup on top. Of course, if you want to top this with crème fraîche, you have my blessing. // TINA

SUN-DRIED TOMATO SOUP

MAKES 8 QUARTS

Heat the oil in the stockpot. Add the onions, carrots, and garlic and sauté for about 7 minutes, or until the vegetables are tender but not brown.

// Add the sun- or oven-dried tomatoes, canned tomatoes, vegetable broth, and half of the basil. Stir in the salt and pepper. Bring to a boil, reduce the heat, and simmer, loosely covered, for 50 minutes.

// Remove the soup from the heat and, using an immersion blender, briefly puree the soup, leaving larger tomato chunks for some texture. After blending, add the sliced scallions. Season with salt and pepper.

FOR DELIVERY
Include one quarter of the remaining basil and of the grilled cheese croutons.

TO SERVE
Reheat the soup and top each bowl with basil and a small handful of the grilled cheese croutons.

COURTNEY: Sometimes I actually forget it is soup day. This tomato soup arrived on one such evening when I was ready to make a meal out of red wine and Melted Cheese Crackers (page 231). When the doorbell rang I hesitated; I wasn't expecting a package or a visitor. To my great delight it was Tina. Smiling ear to ear, she thrust a packed bag of soup and extras into my arms and declared, "I hope you like tomatoes!" and disappeared into the elevator. I was totally stunned and a little speechless. The soup made my evening and I polished off the leftovers at lunch the next day.

Late summer in New York is Crazy Squash Time. The zucchini from our CSA average TWO POUNDS each, they reach a foot in length, with a three-inch diameter, and I wanted to Soup Club them into submission. In Crazy Squash months, I am a devoted fan of Fergus Henderson's Mushy Zucchini, a braise of enormous amounts of sliced squash in enormous amounts of butter and garlic. But I took a cue from my friend Assaf, who has a great touch with fresh herbs and hot peppers, and went for this Mediterranean-Mexican flavor mash-up. Tahini, meet tomatillos. // CAROLINE

SUMMER SQUASH SOUP WITH SALSA FLAVORS

MAKES 8 QUARTS

Preheat the oven to 425°F.

// Spread the combined squash, garlic, and sliced jalapeños onto four large rimmed baking sheets. (You may need to do this in two batches.)

// Drizzle 3 tablespoons of the olive oil over each pan, tossing to coat evenly. Sprinkle the thyme and oregano over the vegetables, then sprinkle ½ teaspoon of the salt and 1 teaspoon of the cumin over each pan. Tuck the tomatillos and whole jalapeños onto the pans wherever you can.

// Roast for 15 minutes, stirring once halfway through. Reduce the temperature to 275°F, and roast for 15 more minutes. Remove the pans from the oven and set aside 4 of the tomatillos and the 4 whole jalapeños, which should be shriveled and deflated by now.

// In the stockpot, heat the remaining 3 tablespoons of olive oil and sauté the onions until soft, about 7 minutes. Add the roasted vegetables to the pot, salt generously, and pour in the broth. Bring to a boil, reduce the heat, and simmer for 10 minutes.

// Turn off the heat, and use an immersion blender to give the soup a partial puree, but be sure to keep it chunky. Season with salt and pepper.

// In a food processor, make a quick salsa verde by pureeing the remaining tomatillos and jalapeños with the lime juice and a big pinch of salt. Stir in half the chopped parsley.

10 pounds **summer squash** (any variety, such as zucchini, pattypan, or crookneck), chopped

3 heads **garlic** (about 30 cloves), smashed

8 **jalapeño peppers** or similar medium-hot peppers, 4 thinly sliced, 4 left whole

¾ to 1 cup **olive oil**, plus 3 tablespoons

6 tablespoons fresh **thyme leaves**

6 tablespoons fresh **oregano leaves**

3 teaspoons **salt**, plus more to taste

4 teaspoons freshly ground **cumin**

8 fresh **tomatillos**, husks removed

5 medium **yellow onions**, quartered and thinly sliced

5 quarts **vegetable broth** or **chicken broth**

Freshly ground **black pepper**

¼ cup freshly squeezed **lime juice** (from about 2 limes)

1 large bunch **flat-leaf parsley**, leaves and top stems only, roughly chopped

1 large bunch **cilantro**

2 cups **tahini**

White Bean–Ramp–Radish Mash (page 227)

16 small **corn tortillas**

FOR DELIVERY

Include one quarter of the salsa verde, parsley, cilantro, tahini, white bean mash, and tortillas.

TO SERVE

Reheat the soup and stir in the tahini (thinned with a little boiling water) just before serving. Top with parsley, cilantro, and salsa verde. Make little tacos with the White Bean-Ramp-Radish Mash wrapped in warmed tortillas to eat alongside.

JULIE: I went through a bizarre culinary phase where I impulsively added peanut butter to nearly every soup I made. So, when Tina announced she was making Senegalese Peanut Soup, I was thrilled. Tina gets the flavors just right here, a perfect balance of sweet and spicy, creamy and chunky. I add sautéed shrimp for a little something extra.

My husband and I had dinner one night with old friends. They are fantastic home cooks, so I asked if they had made any memorable soups lately. "Yes! Senegalese Peanut Soup." The flavors they described—peanuts, coconut, ginger, tomato, sweet potato—appealed immediately. On our rainy cab ride home, I found myself sitting in the front seat of the taxi and it turned out that the driver was Senegalese. He and I talked peanuts and cooking, and he heartily confirmed that a soup rich with peanuts and sweet potatoes is a beloved traditional meal in his country. He also explained that while raw peanuts are widely available in Senegal, store-bought roasted ones are a fine substitute here in the States. Carried forward by the serendipitous confluence of events, I made this the following week. // TINA

SENEGALESE PEANUT SOUP

MAKES 8 QUARTS

Roughly crush the peanuts using the side of a large knife or put them in a zipper bag and smash them with a rolling pin or bottle.

// Peel and finely mince 4 ounces of the ginger.

// Heat the oil in the stockpot. Add the onions, garlic, and minced ginger. Sauté until soft, about 7 minutes. Add the salt, curry powder, and red pepper flakes and cook for a few minutes, until the spices are aromatic.

// Stir in the diced tomatoes, then add 2 cups of the peanuts. Cook for another few minutes, stirring frequently to prevent burning.

// Add the sweet potatoes, 3½ quarts water, and the coconut milk. Chop half of one bunch of cilantro and add it to the stockpot. Bring the soup to a boil, reduce the heat, and simmer for about 20 minutes, loosely covered, until the sweet potatoes are just tender.

// Remove the soup from the heat. Ladle out 3 quarts of soup and set aside; be sure to include some sweet potato and tomato chunks since this portion will remain unblended.

// Add the peanut butter to the stockpot and use an immersion blender to puree the soup until the peanut butter is well incorporated. Return the unblended portion to the stockpot, add the spinach, and stir to combine. Season with salt and pepper.

NOTE: *If halving this recipe, you can still use the entire can of unsweetened coconut milk.*

4 cups roasted, **salted peanuts**

8 ounces fresh **ginger**, divided

¼ cup **peanut**, **coconut**, or **canola oil**, or a combination

3 medium **red onions**, quartered and thinly sliced

1 head of **garlic** (about 10 cloves), peeled and crushed

1 tablespoon **salt**, plus more to taste

¼ cup mild **curry powder**

½ teaspoon **red pepper flakes** (optional)

2 28-ounce cans diced **tomatoes**, with their juice

5 large **sweet potatoes**, peeled and roughly cut into 1-inch cubes (about 5 pounds)

1 13.5-ounce can unsweetened **coconut milk**, well stirred

2 bunches **cilantro**, divided

1 cup unsweetened **peanut butter**

8 ounces baby **spinach**

Freshly ground **black pepper**

FOR DELIVERY

Include one quarter of the remaining peanuts, cilantro, and ginger.

TO SERVE

Reheat the soup. Grate fresh ginger into the pot or directly into the soup bowl when eating. Top with more peanuts and chopped cilantro leaves.

¼ cup **olive oil**

3 medium **yellow onions**, chopped

1 head of **garlic** (about 10 cloves), minced

3 tablespoons ground **cumin**

3 tablespoons ground **coriander**

1 teaspoon **red pepper flakes**

1 tablespoon **salt**, plus more to taste

1 pound **carrots**, chopped into ½-inch cubes

2 pounds **sweet potatoes** (about 2 large), peeled and chopped into ½-inch cubes

2 pounds **red potatoes** (8 to 10), scrubbed and cut into ½-inch cubes

2 pounds **butternut squash** (about 4 cups), peeled and cut into ½-inch cubes

4 15.5-ounce cans **chickpeas**, drained

6 quarts **vegetable broth**

3 **cinnamon** sticks

2 bunches **flat-leaf parsley**

3 bunches **cilantro**, divided

Honey (optional)

Freshly ground **black pepper**

8 cups cooked **couscous**

Bennah and I grew up in Los Angeles together and our lives have been linked ever since: Her mom was my high school Spanish teacher; I went to Shabbat dinner every Friday night at her house; we are neighbors now in New York City and our kids are like siblings. When vacationing together last summer, I asked Bennah to make soup with me, something from the Moroccan Jewish side of her family. After a text to one cousin in Florida and an e-mail to another in France, we devised a soup based on a Moroccan seven-vegetable dish that is traditionally served over couscous. Everyone on our trip, which included reluctant eaters, kids and adults, enjoyed this soup. The adults added some heat, but that was it. // TINA

MOROCCAN CORIANDER VEGETABLE SOUP

MAKES 8 QUARTS

Heat the oil in the stockpot and sauté the onions for about 7 minutes, or until soft. Add the garlic, cumin, coriander, red pepper flakes, and salt and cook for another few minutes, stirring constantly.

// Add the carrots, sweet potatoes, red potatoes, squash, chickpeas, broth, and cinnamon sticks. Using kitchen twine, tie together the 2 bunches of parsley and 2 bunches of the cilantro (reserving one for delivery). Add the bundles to the soup and bring to a boil. Reduce the heat and simmer, loosely covered, for 1 hour.

// Remove the bundles of herbs and the cinnamon sticks. Taste and stir in honey, if desired. Season with salt and pepper.

FOR DELIVERY
Include one quarter of the reserved cilantro and 2 cups of the couscous.

TO SERVE
Reheat the soup and the couscous. Ladle the soup over couscous in each soup bowl. Top with chopped cilantro leaves.

10 medium **red beets** (about 5 pounds), scrubbed

¼ cup **neutral oil**

2 medium **yellow onions**, chopped

2 tablespoons **salt**, plus more to taste

1½ tablespoons **caraway seeds**

1 28-ounce can crushed **tomatoes**

1 6-ounce can **tomato paste**

1 pound **carrots**, chopped into ½-inch cubes

2 pounds **waxy potatoes** (about 6 medium), such as Yukon Gold, peeled and chopped into ½-inch cubes

1 small head **white cabbage** (about 1½ pounds), shredded and cut into 1-inch pieces (about 6 cups)

4½ quarts **vegetable broth**

6 **bay leaves**

1 bunch **flat-leaf parsley**, stems tied together

White vinegar, up to ½ cup (Yes, I vote for vinegar)

Brown sugar

Freshly ground **black pepper**

8 hard-boiled **eggs**

1 loaf dark **rye bread**

16 ounces **sour cream**

1 large bunch **dill**

CHILLED BORSCHT Puree 1 quart borscht, 1 cup plain, unsweetened kefir, 1 finely minced garlic clove, and 1 to 2 tablespoons seasoned rice vinegar in an upright blender. Top with diced cucumber, thinly sliced radish, fresh chopped dill, and half a hard-boiled egg.

Borscht is eaten in most Russian homes, and every Russian I spoke with advocates good-heartedly for their own variation of beets, onions, carrots, cabbage, and tomatoes. But adding vinegar to borscht can be controversial, if not downright divisive. For some, it is an essential part of striking the right balance between sweet and sour in the soup. For others, it is a big no-no. I queried the man behind the deli counter: "Vinegar?" He replied: "Of course, and it needs to be white, absolutely. I know; I am Russian." When a woman in the grocery store talked me through her recipe without mention of vinegar, I asked, "Vinegar?" "Of course not!" she said emphatically. "Who told you to add vinegar?" *Priyatnova apetita!* // TINA

BORSCHT

MAKES 8 QUARTS

Cover the beets with water in a 4- to 6-quart pot and bring to a boil. Reduce the heat and simmer for about 30 minutes, or until you can easily stick a fork into the flesh. Drain the beets, trim off the root ends, and remove their skins with a paring knife. Cut the beets into ½-inch cubes. This can be done a day or two in advance.

// In the stockpot, heat the oil and sauté the onions for 7 minutes, or until soft. Stir in the salt and caraway seeds. Continue to cook for another few minutes, until fragrant.

// Add the crushed tomatoes, tomato paste, carrots, potatoes, cabbage, broth, bay leaves, parsley, and the beets and bring to a boil. Reduce the heat and simmer, loosely covered, for 40 to 50 minutes, or until all the vegetables are tender.

// Add 1 tablespoon of the vinegar and taste the broth. You want the right balance of sweet and sour. Add brown sugar and additional vinegar until you get there. Season with salt and pepper.

FOR DELIVERY	TO SERVE
Include one quarter of the hard-boiled eggs, bread, sour cream, and dill.	Peel and halve the eggs. Reheat the soup and top with a dollop of sour cream, chopped dill, and ½ hard-boiled egg. Serve alongside buttered bread.

// Add the shredded squash, the rest of the broth, and a pinch of cayenne pepper. Bring to a boil, reduce the heat, and simmer for 20 more minutes, loosely covered. Add a little more grated turmeric if desired, and season with salt and pepper. Remove the lemongrass bundle before delivering and serving.

FOR DELIVERY

Portion the tofu croutons into each jar before ladling in the soup. This ensures even distribution, and the tofu absorbs the soup's flavor as it sits. Include one quarter of the remaining turmeric and 2 cups of the rice.

TO SERVE

Reheat the soup and rice. Add a scoop of rice to each bowl, then the soup. Finish with a drizzle of sesame oil, more freshly grated turmeric, and Sriracha.

> **JULIE:** When Caroline thoughtfully left this soup at my door the morning after my 103°F fever, I experienced firsthand its healing anti-inflammatory properties. The ginger, garlic, turmeric, and greens tasted so good together. Per Caroline's suggestion, I added more Sriracha to the soup than I normally do and was on my way to wellness that very afternoon.

With a soup like this, the **COOKING TIME** will depend mostly on how happy you are with the flavor. The leafy greens will continue to break down as they sit in the broth, and there's no danger of undercooking. If you like the flavor, then it's done.

4 tablespoons **olive oil**

6 **carrots**, roughly chopped

3 medium **onions**, roughly chopped

1 head of **garlic** (about 10 cloves), chopped

6 **celery stalks**, chopped

1 tablespoon dried **oregano**

2 tablespoons **fennel seeds**, crushed

3 **fennel bulbs**, white parts finely sliced, fronds finely chopped and reserved

5 28-ounce cans whole peeled **tomatoes**, with their juice

2 whole sprigs **rosemary**, tied with kitchen twine

3 **bay leaves**

7 cups cooked **chickpeas** (from 1 pound dried), cooking liquid reserved (may be made up to 2 days in advance)

½ cup **red wine** (optional)

2 tablespoons **salt**, plus more to taste

Freshly ground **black pepper**

2 cups **Crème Fraîche** (page 47)

Pesto (page 44), made with kale, parsley, and fennel fronds or with basil and pine nuts

Red pepper flakes, for serving

Amanda's Grilled Cheese Croutons (page 43)

NOTE You need 2 quarts of cooking liquid to add to the soup. If you're short, make up the difference with water.

I love black licorice and anise-flavored anything, so fennel is kind of my dream vegetable. As an alternative to pesto, crumble in blue cheese at the end, like the salty-creamy Bleu d'Auvergne. This soup falls squarely into the ". . . Or Maybe It's a Sauce" category, and my kids prefer it over pasta. // CAROLINE

TOMATO-FENNEL-CHICKPEA SOUP

MAKES 8 QUARTS

In a stockpot, heat the oil and sauté the carrots, onions, garlic, and celery for 7 minutes, or until soft. Add the oregano, fennel seeds, and two thirds of the sliced fennel. Cook over medium heat for about 10 minutes, until the fennel is soft.

// Add the tomatoes, rosemary, bay leaves, 2 quarts of the chickpea cooking liquid, wine, if using, and the salt. Bring to a boil, reduce the heat, and simmer for 40 minutes, loosely covered. Remove the soup from the heat and fish out the rosemary sprigs and bay leaves. Puree the soup with an immersion blender until smooth.

// Add the remaining sliced fennel and the chickpeas. Simmer for 15 minutes, or until the fennel is tender but still crisp. If the soup is too thick, add water as desired. Season with salt and pepper.

FOR DELIVERY	TO SERVE
Include one quarter of the crème fraîche, pesto, and grilled cheese croutons.	Reheat the soup and top each bowl with a dollop each of crème fraîche and pesto and a big pinch of red pepper flakes— the Italian *tricolore* in a bowl. Pass around the croutons for dotting on top.

CHILLED

Soup is a four-season food, and these are for the warm days, when you don't want to turn on your stove. Take advantage of summer fruits and vegetables and turn them into chilled soups: They are refreshing, quick, and easy to prepare for a light dinner. Make chilled soups a few hours before serving to allow the flavors to deepen and for the soup to get nice and cold. Cold dulls flavors, though, so taste the soup again when chilled through and add lemon, lime, or additional salt and herbs to enhance the flavors before serving.

Soup Club tends to disperse a bit in the summers, but we've all learned that even the most sparsely furnished summer rental comes with a blender, and if you can make a frozen margarita, you can make a chilled soup.

When I think of the heat in the Los Angeles Valley in August, I want to make this soup . . . even if it's a snowy day in January on the East Coast. Unlike the seasonally available ingredients in many chilled soups, cucumbers are available year-round. So go ahead and indulge when the urge arises. // TINA

CUCUMBER-YOGURT SOUP

MAKES 8 QUARTS

Peel, seed, and roughly chop 16 of the cucumbers. Peel the remaining 2 cucumbers. Cut them lengthwise, then seed and slice them into half-moons and set aside for delivery.

// Put 2 cups of the walnuts, the 16 chopped cucumbers, 2 quarts of the Greek yogurt, the scallions, garlic, mint, parsley, the minced dill, the lemon zest and juice, and the ice-cold water or broth in the stockpot. Using an immersion blender (and some muscle), blend until very smooth. Add a little additional chilled water as needed to get it all going. Season with salt and pepper.

// Refrigerate for at least 2 hours before serving, or until thoroughly chilled.

18 medium **cucumbers** (about 9 pounds), divided

6 cups **walnuts**, toasted and then roughly chopped (see page 50), divided

2½ quarts plain **Greek yogurt**, divided

4 **scallions**, green and white parts, chopped

4 **garlic cloves**, minced

2 cups fresh **mint** leaves

2 cups fresh **flat-leaf parsley** leaves

1 bunch **dill**, ½ cup minced

Grated zest of 1 **lemon** plus 1 cup freshly squeezed **lemon juice** (from 6 to 8 **lemons**)

3 cups ice-cold **water**, or cold **Vegetable Broth** (page 30), plus more as needed

Salt and freshly ground **black pepper**

NOTE It's important to use a **HOMEMADE BROTH** here, because the flavor really comes through.

FOR DELIVERY	TO SERVE
Include one quarter of the remaining walnuts, Greek yogurt, dill, and sliced cucumbers.	Stir half of the walnuts into the soup. Top with fresh dill, a dollop of yogurt, finely sliced cucumber, and more walnuts. Add a splash of hot sauce.

2 medium seedless **watermelons** (about 15 pounds each)

5 medium **shallots**, finely diced

3 **orange bell peppers**, peeled, seeded, and diced into ¼-inch cubes

3 **red bell peppers**, peeled, seeded, and diced into ¼-inch cubes

3 medium **cucumbers**, peeled, seeded, and diced into ¼-inch cubes

3 **garlic cloves**, minced

6 tablespoons **olive oil**

6 tablespoons **red wine vinegar**

6 tablespoons freshly squeezed **lemon juice** (from 3 to 4 lemons)

1 tablespoon **salt**, plus more to taste

1 bunch **flat-leaf parsley**, minced

1 large bunch fresh **basil**, minced

4 small **jalapeño peppers** (optional)

8 6-ounce pieces of **salmon**, cooked and chilled, or 1 pound fresh **mozzarella**, diced

Freshly ground **black pepper**

FOR DELIVERY

Include a jalapeño, if using, and one quarter of the salmon or fresh mozzarella.

TO SERVE

Divide the salmon into bowls and pour the soup over. If using mozzarella, add on top of the soup. Either way, garnish with jalapeño slices if you like. Add black pepper to taste just before serving.

My husband, David, and I like to eat dinner together at home although our work schedules often conspire against us. Sometimes he comes home from work first and starts a meal and I join in the kitchen midway, the resulting dinner a mash-up of our individual concoctions. David's go-to dish is a simple baked salmon and I make a pairing. Braised Leafy Greens with Egg (page 172) or Escarole, Grapefruit, and Hazelnut Salad (page 156) are favorites. We discovered the unexpected combination of watermelon gazpacho and leftover cold salmon when we both dived into the fridge rather than heating up the kitchen on a hot summer night. The salmon bulks up the light soup and the savory salty fish is a good foil to the sweetness of the watermelon and vegetables. If you're not a fish eater, consider diced fresh mozzarella. // COURTNEY

WATERMELON GAZPACHO

MAKES 8 QUARTS

Rinse or wipe the outside of the watermelon so the rind is clean. Cut the flesh from the rind on one watermelon into large pieces, about 15 cups worth. You'll be pureeing them, so cut roughly and dump the chunks into the stockpot.

// Add half of the shallots, bell peppers, and cucumbers to the stockpot, along with all of the garlic.

// Add the olive oil, vinegar, and lemon juice. Using an immersion blender, puree until smooth. The mixture will be pale and frothy. Add 1 tablespoon of the salt.

// Add the parsley and basil to the stockpot. Stir in the reserved shallots, bell peppers, and cucumbers.

// Cut the flesh from the rind of the remaining watermelon, dice into ¼-inch cubes, and add it to the stockpot. I do this by slicing the watermelon into quarters, keeping the flesh on the rind so the pieces can be swept off with the back of a chef's knife into the pot. Stir gently to combine. Salt to taste.

This soup is so rich, a little goes a long way. For Soup Club, I delivered only one quart, pairing it with one quart of the Tomato Gazpacho (page 120). Try swirling them together, or use this soup as a bed (or sauce) for grilled fish or strips of garlic-rubbed flank steak. You can caramelize the onions a day in advance, but the soup is best made the day you want to serve it. // CAROLINE

AVOCADO-ARUGULA SOUP

MAKES 8 QUARTS

Heat the oil and butter in a frying pan and sauté the onions over medium heat for about 20 minutes, or until they start to brown and caramelize. Remove from the heat and let cool.

// Halve and pit each avocado. Scoop out the avocado flesh into the stockpot (I use a spoon for this), and combine with the onions, jalapeños, arugula, cilantro, parsley, oregano, garlic, coriander, cumin, lime juice, broth, yogurt, salt, and pepper.

// Using an immersion blender, puree the soup until smooth. Check for seasoning, adding extra lime juice, salt, and pepper to taste. The texture should be thick but pourable. If it's too thick, thin with a bit of cold water. To thicken, add another dollop of Greek yogurt, up to ½ cup.

// Refrigerate immediately, and chill for at least 4 hours. Add extra lime juice just before serving.

FOR DELIVERY
Include 1 lime and one quarter of the chili-lime pepitas and crostini or chips.

TO SERVE
Sprinkle each bowl liberally with pepitas. Serve with lime wedges and crostini or chips on the side.

1 tablespoon **olive oil**

1 tablespoon **butter**

4 medium **yellow onions**, thinly sliced into half-moons

12 ripe **avocados**

4 **jalapeño peppers**, seeded and finely chopped

1 pound **arugula**

2 cups loosely packed fresh **cilantro** leaves

1 cup loosely packed fresh **flat-leaf parsley** leaves

2 tablespoons fresh **oregano** leaves

2 **garlic cloves**, minced

2 teaspoons ground **coriander**

3 teaspoons ground **cumin**

⅓ cup freshly squeezed **lime juice** (from 4 to 6 limes), plus more to taste

4 quarts **Vegetable Broth** (page 30) or **Chicken Broth** (page 30)

2 cups plain **Greek yogurt**, plus more to taste

2 tablespoons **salt**, plus more to taste

2 teaspoons freshly ground **black pepper**, plus more to taste

4 **limes**

Chili-Lime Pepitas (page 51)

Crostini (page 179) or **tortilla chips**

NOTE It's important to use a **HOMEMADE BROTH** here, because the flavor really comes through.

MELON
&
MINT

WATERMELON
GAZPACHO

CURRIED
GREEN PEA
&
SPINACH

12 **celery stalks**, chopped

3 large **green bell peppers**, cored, seeded, and chopped

2 **zucchini**, peeled and chopped

7 pounds **cucumbers**, peeled and diced (about 14 cups)

2 jalapeño **peppers**, seeded and diced

1 head of **garlic** (about 10 cloves), minced

4 teaspoons **sugar**

1 cup **olive oil**

4 cups unsweetened **almond milk**

4 cups sliced blanched **almonds**, lightly toasted

3 bunches **spinach** (30 ounces), cleaned and stems removed

4 cups loosely packed **basil leaves**, stems removed

4 cups loosely packed fresh **flat-leaf parsley leaves**, stems removed

Grated zest and juice of 4 **lemons**

1 cup **sherry vinegar**

4 cups plain **Greek yogurt**, plus 4 single-serving (6- to 7-ounce) containers plain Greek yogurt reserved for delivery

3 tablespoons **salt**, plus more to taste

2 teaspoons **white pepper**, plus more to taste

Basic Croutons (page 43)

12 to 16 **breakfast radishes**, thinly sliced

BABY CUCUMBERS, if you can find them, are sweeter and more flavorful than the giant ones.

You can substitute **BAGGED BABY SPINACH**, but reduce to 20 ounces, because you use all of it. You lose a lot of weight removing stems from large spinach bunches.

There are usually eighteen of us gathered at my parents' house for our summer reunion. One recent July, there was an abundance of green peppers and cucumbers lying on the kitchen counter, and making a green gazpacho seemed like the perfect way to use them up and feed our big group. My cold-soup–averse family gave it a try, and with those green vegetables and herbs at their finest, this zingy puree won them over.

Serve it with Jeweled Rice (page 192), Tomato-Watermelon Salad (page 155), or Corn and Red Pepper Salad (page 159) and add grilled salmon for a full dinner. Or eat it alone for a light lunch on a steamy summer afternoon. Definitely serve with a cocktail. // JULIE

GREEN GAZPACHO

MAKES 8 QUARTS

Place the celery, green peppers, zucchini, cucumbers, jalapeños, and garlic in the stockpot. Add the sugar, olive oil, and almond milk along with 1 quart cold water, and puree with an immersion blender until smooth.

// Add the toasted almonds, spinach, basil, parsley, lemon zest and juice, vinegar, yogurt, salt, and white pepper, and blend until well combined. You can't get it silky smooth with an immersion blender, but you'll get to use your upright blender just before serving. Add more water if you prefer a thinner consistency. Season with salt and pepper.

// Refrigerate for 4 hours or until thoroughly chilled before eating.

FOR DELIVERY	**TO SERVE**
Include 1 single-serving container of yogurt, and one quarter of the croutons and radishes.	Transfer the soup to an upright blender and blend to a smooth consistency. Serve with a dollop of yogurt and top with a handful of croutons and a few thin radish slices.

This soup is utter refreshment on a hot day. I heartily thank my chef-friend and running partner Carlin for sharing the idea of this soup with me while we were sweating it out together one morning. Great for breakfast after a long run, its sweet, gingery, and slightly salty flavor has the power to magically replenish an exercise-weary body. // JULIE

MELON AND MINT SOUP

MAKES 8 QUARTS

16 **limes**, divided, with 12 of them juiced

4 to 5 large ripe **cantaloupes** (about 25 pounds), peeled, membranes discarded and melon roughly chopped (36 to 40 cups)

2 cups plain **Greek yogurt**, plus 4 single-serving (6- to 7-ounce) containers for delivery

3 tablespoons grated peeled fresh **ginger**

2 teaspoons **salt**, plus more to taste

4 cups loosely packed fresh **mint leaves** (about 2 big bunches), roughly chopped and divided

6 to 8 **scallions**, white and green parts, roughly chopped

Add the juice, cantaloupe, the 2 cups of yogurt, ginger, salt, half of the mint leaves, and all the scallions to the stockpot. Puree with an immersion blender until smooth. If the soup is too thick, thin with cold water to the desired consistency.

// Refrigerate until chilled, then add salt to taste. If serving the soup right away, add a few ice cubes to chill and blend again until smooth.

FOR DELIVERY

Include 1 lime, 1 single-serving container of yogurt, and one quarter of the remaining mint.

TO SERVE

Garnish the chilled soup with a dollop of yogurt, a pinch of mint leaves, and a wedge of lime. Eat as a soup or pour into a glass and drink like a smoothie.

TEQUILA MELON FIZZ

My brother Tom, the self-appointed family mixologist, is in charge of cocktail hour when we're together. His drinks tend to start with lime juice and they take advantage of fresh herbs. This is one of Tom's recent inventions for warm summer evenings.

For each cocktail, combine in a cocktail shaker 2 parts watermelon juice, 1 part freshly squeezed lime juice, 2 parts tequila, and a few mint leaves. Add a pinch of salt, several ice cubes, and shake to combine. Strain into a glass and top with a splash of bubbly, seltzer, or prosecco. Garnish with a wedge of lime and fresh mint leaves.

4 large hothouse (also called English) **cucumbers**, peeled and diced (about 6½ cups)

4 **red bell peppers**, cored, seeded, and diced

4 pounds **tomatoes**, peeled and chopped

8 **celery stalks**, diced

8 **scallions**, green and white parts, finely sliced

3 **garlic cloves**, minced

1 bunch **flat-leaf parsley**, leaves only, chopped

2 teaspoons **Worcestershire sauce**

½ cup **sherry vinegar**

8 tablespoons good **olive oil**

4 quarts **vegetable** or **tomato juice**

4 teaspoons **salt**, plus more to taste

1 teaspoon freshly ground **black pepper**, plus more to taste

Hot pepper sauce

White Bean–Ramp–Radish Mash (page 227) or **Baba Ghanoush** (page 225)

1 16-ounce bag **corn tortilla chips**

TO PEEL TOMATOES: Have ready a pot of boiling water and a bowl of ice water. Cut a small X into the bottom of each tomato, and plunge them into the boiling water for 30 seconds, then into the ice water. Once they are cool enough to touch, the skins will slip off easily.

Growing up, I loved going through my mother's cookbooks and recipe-card library. There were lots of fascinating jellied "salads" and canned-food casseroles, not that there's anything wrong with that (see Corn Casserole, page 187), but also this—a classic tomato gazpacho with a garden's worth of fresh vegetables. All the work is in chopping them up, so it's good for practicing your knife skills without getting overwhelmed by other techniques. This is best made in peak tomato season. // CAROLINE

TOMATO GAZPACHO

MAKES 8 QUARTS

Combine the cucumbers, bell peppers, tomatoes, celery, scallions, garlic, parsley, Worcestershire sauce, vinegar, olive oil, vegetable juice, salt, and pepper in the stockpot. Chill in the refrigerator for at least 4 hours before serving, and season again with salt and pepper if needed.

FOR DELIVERY
Include one quarter of the white bean-ramp-radish mash, baba ghanoush, and the chips.

TO SERVE
Like most chilled soups, this looks pretty in a glass bowl, but that's optional. Drizzle with hot sauce. Serve chips and white bean mash on the side, scooping and dipping with abandon.

FISH

Fish soups feel like a special treat for Soup Club. Maybe that's because fish costs more than beans and squash, plus there are a lot of questions that arise before purchasing: Is it local? Low in mercury? Sustainable? If you don't have access to a good fishmonger, there are lots of online resources to guide your seafood buying (seafoodwatch.org is one reliable site). And if you're in a landlocked area, check out your grocery's freezer section: Flash-frozen fish can often be the best, freshest choice you make. These four recipes are great entry-level soups for the fish novice, so dive in.

Nico, my oldest child, is starting to show a real interest in cooking. When he was five, my husband and I read *Harry Potter and the Sorcerer's Stone* to him. He listened closely and got the gist of it, but when we reached the part about the Mirror of Erised we slowed down to make sure that he really understood. This magical mirror reveals your greatest desire, rather than your actual reflection, and as parents we recognized our opportunity to sneak a peek into the soul of our son. My husband asked Nico what he would see if he looked in the Mirror of Erised, and Nico answered without hesitation: "I would see myself eating delicious bread with soft butter in front of the TV." He totally got it.

I dedicate this soup to Nico . . . to enjoy alongside his deliciously buttered bread, which really is this salmon soup's best accompaniment. // TINA

SALMON SOUP IN WHITE BROTH

MAKES 8 QUARTS

Heat the butter in the stockpot over medium heat. Add the leeks and onions and cook for 8 to 10 minutes, until soft. Stir occasionally to prevent browning. Stir in 2 tablespoons of the salt along with the carrots, celery, and potatoes.

// Add the vegetable broth, bay leaves, and white pepper, and bring the soup to a boil. Reduce the heat and simmer for 6 to 8 minutes, loosely covered, until the potatoes are almost tender.

// Add the salmon and cook for 2 minutes, or until the flesh is nearly firm and opaque. Stir in the final tablespoon of salt, and remove from the heat. Let sit for 5 minutes.

// Stir half of the dill into the soup, along with the cream. Discard the bay leaves. Season with salt and black pepper.

4 tablespoons (½ stick) **butter**

4 **leeks**, trimmed and cleaned (white and pale green parts only; reserve the dark green tops for broth), cut into thin rounds

3 medium **red onions**, quartered and thinly sliced

3 tablespoons **salt**, plus more to taste

1 pound **carrots** (about 8), halved lengthwise and thinly sliced into half-rounds

4 **celery stalks**, finely diced

4 pounds small **red potatoes** (12 to 15), scrubbed, unpeeled and diced

6 quarts **vegetable broth**

6 **bay leaves**

1 teaspoon freshly ground **white pepper**

3 pounds skinless, boneless **salmon fillets**, cut into bite-size cubes

2 bunches **dill**, leaves only, finely chopped

1 pint **heavy cream**

Freshly ground **black pepper**

Large loaf of **crusty wheat** or **rye bread**

FOR DELIVERY
Include one quarter of the remaining dill and one quarter of the bread.

TO SERVE
Gently reheat the soup without boiling, and top with dill. Serve with a side of bread and butter.

---

5 medium **sweet potatoes** (about 4 pounds), peeled and diced into ½-inch cubes

¼ cup **olive oil**

3 medium **yellow onions**, chopped

4 ounces fresh **ginger**, peeled and finely chopped (about ¾ cup)

1 head of **garlic** (about 10 cloves), minced

8 13.5-ounce cans unsweetened **coconut milk**, well stirred

1 6.8-ounce jar **Thai red curry paste**

1 quart **vegetable broth** or fish broth

½ cup plus 2 tablespoons **fish sauce**

8 **limes**, 4 zested

2 pounds **green beans**, trimmed and cut in half

3 pounds **tilapia** or other mild white fish, cut into bite-size chunks

20 to 25 ounces fresh **baby spinach** (I always use bagged to make my life easier)

5 cups packed fresh **basil leaves**

Soy sauce or **tamari**

Red pepper flakes

2 cups **peanuts**, finely chopped

8 cups cooked **jasmine rice**

This recipe was a bit of a breakthrough for me. It demonstrated that you really can capture much of Thai cuisine's exotic piquancy with the incorporation of a competent, store-bought red curry paste, good spices, and enough coconut milk. It tastes much more labor intensive and complicated than it is. Increase the spice with curry paste or a pinch or two of red pepper flakes if desired.

The fish can make this soup a bit wallet-busting, but tilapia is a pretty economical choice. Substitute Coconut Wheat Berries with Herbs (page 195) in place of the jasmine rice if you'd like. // JULIE

THAI FISH CURRY

MAKES 8 QUARTS

Bring 2 cups water to boil in a large pot and add the sweet potatoes. Reduce the heat to a simmer, cover, and cook for 10 minutes, or until just tender. Remove from the heat and strain in a colander over a medium bowl, reserving the liquid. Note: Be careful not to overcook the sweet potatoes in this step or they will turn to mush and fall apart.

// Meanwhile, heat the oil in the stockpot and sauté the onions, ginger, and garlic until soft, about 7 minutes.

// Add 1 can of the coconut milk and whisk in the red curry paste until the clumps of paste have dissolved. Add the remaining coconut milk, the broth, fish sauce, and the lime zest and bring to a boil before reducing to a simmer.

// Add the green beans and fish. Cook for 7 to 10 minutes, or until the fish is opaque and flakes easily when pierced with a fork.

// Add the spinach, sweet potatoes, and 3 cups of the basil. Stir until well combined. Add a few dashes of soy sauce and a large pinch or two of red pepper flakes to taste.

FOR DELIVERY	TO SERVE
Include 1 lime and one quarter of the remaining basil, the peanuts, and the rice.	Reheat the soup and serve over rice. Top with peanuts, basil, and a wedge of lime.

This was a staple of dinner parties my husband and I hosted when we first ventured into vaguely grown-up entertaining. Most memorably, it was the main course at a New Year's Eve gathering that was originally intended for six people, but somehow grew into fourteen. I can't remember how we sat and ate together at our dining table, but I know we did. That's the beauty of soups in general: What was intended for a smallish group can end up feeding a largish one, and is suitable for the most festive or quotidian of meals.

Prepare the tomato-saffron base a day in advance, if possible. This gets the lion's share of the cooking out of the way, and the flavors get even better with some time to sit and mingle. // CAROLINE

SAFFRON SEAFOOD CHOWDER

MAKES 8 QUARTS

¼ cup **olive oil**

6 large **leeks**, trimmed, cleaned, and finely sliced (also okay to substitute a combination of shallots and red onions, 3 pounds total, finely chopped)

6 **garlic cloves**, finely chopped

6 **celery stalks**, finely chopped

1 tablespoon **salt**, plus more to taste

Large pinch of **saffron threads**

1 tablespoon dried **oregano**

1 tablespoon **fennel seeds**, crushed

1 tablespoon **red pepper flakes**

4 28-ounce cans diced **tomatoes**, with their juice

3 quarts **fish broth**, **chicken broth**, or **vegetable broth**

½ cup dry **white wine**

16 red or white new **potatoes**, approximately 2 pounds, cut into bite-size pieces

Freshly ground **black pepper**

3 pounds mixed raw **fish fillets** and/or **shellfish** (for example: 1 pound each wild cod, halibut, and tiny bay scallops or monkfish, tilapia, and shrimp), cut into bite-size chunks

1 bunch **flat-leaf parsley**, finely chopped

2 cups **Crème Fraîche** (page 47)

Sourdough bread

Heat the oil in the stockpot and sauté the leeks, garlic, and celery for 7 minutes, until soft. Add the salt, saffron, oregano, fennel seeds, and red pepper flakes and cook for 5 more minutes, until aromatic.

// Add the tomatoes and their juice, the broth, and the wine. Bring to a boil, reduce the heat, and simmer, loosely covered, for 15 minutes. Add the potatoes and continue to simmer for another 15 minutes. Season with salt and pepper, and a little more crushed fennel seed or saffron threads if desired. Let cool and refrigerate until needed for up to 2 days.

FOR DELIVERY

Pack the raw fish separately. Include one quarter of the chopped parsley, crème fraîche, and sourdough bread.

TO SERVE

Bring the tomato base to a simmer, and add the raw fish. Cook for 5 to 7 minutes, until the fish is done. Stir in the crème fraîche and serve immediately. Top each bowl with chopped parsley, a drizzle of fancy olive oil, and a sprinkling of red pepper flakes. Serve with toasted sourdough.

A scallop is always better if it's a little undercooked and should be added to the pot last, if using. If the fish needs more time to cook after the initial 5 minutes, check every minute to ensure it doesn't overcook.

10 fresh **lemongrass stalks**, about 2 pounds

3 cups **mirin** (Japanese cooking wine)

3 ounces fresh **ginger**, peeled and finely chopped

6 **garlic cloves**, minced

6 medium **yellow onions**, chopped

3 cups dry **white wine**

6 13.5-ounce cans unsweetened **coconut milk**, well stirred

2 6.8-ounce jars **Thai green curry paste**

3 quarts **vegetable broth** or **fish broth**

2 cups **heavy cream**

2 cups **milk**

4 pounds **carrots**, sliced into ¼-inch rounds

2 bunches (20 ounces) **greens** (Swiss chard, kale, or dandelion greens), chopped

½ cup **soy sauce** or **tamari**

8 **plantains**, peeled and sliced lengthwise into ¼-inch slices

Peanut oil, for frying

Salt

12 cups cooked **sushi rice**

2 pounds **scallops**

2 bunches **cilantro**

8 medium **tomatoes**

8 **avocados**

8 **limes**

My first soup club was several years ago with friends Julie, Gretchen, and Klaudia, who I met in a neighborhood moms' group. One week, Julie impressed us all with this soup highlighting scallops and including unexpected accompaniments. That soup club only lasted the length of the school year, as our kids moved on to other schools and Julie's family moved away. This soup reminds me of that special group. // JULIE

GREEN COCONUT CURRY WITH SCALLOPS AND FRIED PLANTAINS

MAKES 8 QUARTS

Discard the outer leaves from the lemongrass and trim the root ends and the upper few inches of stalk. Pound each stalk with a wooden spoon or mallet to release the lemon flavor. Put the lemongrass, mirin, ginger, garlic, and onions into the stockpot over medium-high heat and bring to a boil. Reduce the heat and simmer uncovered until the liquid reduces by half, 12 to 15 minutes.

// Add the wine and simmer for 10 minutes while the liquid continues to reduce. Add the coconut milk and whisk in the green curry until incorporated. Add the broth, cream, milk, and carrots. Bring to a boil, reduce the heat, and simmer, loosely covered, until the carrots are tender, about 20 minutes.

// Remove from the heat and fish out the lemongrass stalks. Stir in the greens and soy sauce to taste.

// Pan-fry the plantains in oil over high heat until golden brown, about 1 minute on each side. Remove to a plate lined with paper towels and sprinkle with salt. Set aside and let cool.

FOR DELIVERY

Include one quarter of the cooked rice, fried plantains, scallops, cilantro, tomatoes, avocados, and limes.

TO SERVE

Reheat the curry. Season the scallops with salt and pepper and sear over high heat in butter for about 2 minutes per side, until golden. Fill each bowl with a mound of rice. Ladle in the curry and top with scallops, cilantro leaves, chopped tomato, chopped avocado, plantains, and a wedge of lime. Add Sriracha or red pepper flakes for extra spice.

MEAT

Although Soup Club stayed vegetarian through several rotations, we eventually incorporated our favorite meat-based recipes (Tina, our lone vegetarian, gave her blessing, as her husband and kids are omnivores). In the colder months, these warm our homes and satisfy a craving for something meatier, like meat. Chicken soup has an essential comfort quality, perhaps in every culinary tradition. Sausage complements sturdy winter greens. Ground meat variations deserve their own cookbook, but chili and meatballs are both worthy starting points. We encourage you to seek out and support butchers whose meat comes from humanely raised animals. This is often more expensive than factory-farmed meat. But in the long run, it's better for us and our planet to choose higher-quality meat, enjoyed in smaller quantities and less frequently.

3 tablespoons **neutral oil**

2 tablespoons **salt**, plus more to taste

3 pounds **chicken thighs**, preferably bone-in and skin-on (more fat=more flavor)

3 large **yellow onions**, roughly chopped

4 heads **garlic** (about 40 large cloves), chopped (or simply way, way more than you think you should use)

1 pound fresh **ginger**, peeled and finely chopped (or even more; see headnote)

6 **celery stalks**, diced (about 3 cups)

6 **carrots**, sliced into medium rounds

3 tablespoons **soy sauce**

Cayenne pepper (optional)

2½ cups **short-grain white** or **brown rice**

1 teaspoon ground **white pepper**, or to taste

6 quarts **chicken broth**, **water**, or a combination of the two

2 ounces fresh **turmeric** root (optional)

Last-Minute Greens: 8 cups of spinach, kale, and/or arugula leaves, washed and dried

8 **scallions**, chopped

1 bunch **cilantro**, chopped

Sesame oil, toasted or hot

Sriracha

This is the first soup I ever made by myself. My college friend Miranda taught me when we went to physical theater school in Paris, after graduation. Perhaps unsurprisingly, Parisian clowns in the mid-1990s were an enthusiastically unhealthy breed. I adhered to the four basic food groups of cigarettes, coffee, cheese, and wine; my primary exercise was vigorous pantomime. After a few months, my whole body needed a reboot, and the first time I tasted this soup in Miranda's tiny two-burner kitchen, I felt the wellness returning. It was full of flavor, comfort, and the mythological powers of chicken broth, though it isn't the traditional Jewish Chicken Noodle Soup (page 135). This is Filipino Healing Soup, which resembles Chinese congee and Dominican "soupy rice," and it is the ur-text of my soup-sharing narrative.

The way I most often begin the recipe for friends who ask is "Chop up way more garlic and ginger than you think you should," and I've never made a small batch with less than a whole head of garlic and at least a couple big fingers of ginger. Indeed, it is also referred to as Filipino Chicken Ginger Soup, and the ginger is the star of the show. I fell in love with its spicy warmth and with the super-soothing nature of long-cooked rice punctuated by tender chunks of chicken, powerful medicine to combat physical and emotional malaise.

Today's clowns-in-training probably follow a healthier regimen, but they may still get homesick once in a while—even if it's for someone else's home, someone else's childhood recipe—and this soup is for them. // CAROLINE

FILIPINO HEALING SOUP

MAKES 8 QUARTS

Heat the oil in the stockpot. Use about 1 tablespoon of the salt to season the chicken and brown for about 2 minutes on each side, working in batches. Remove the chicken from the pot and set aside.

// Add the onions, garlic, ginger, celery, and carrots to the pot. Stir them around to coat them in the oil, and cook until soft, about 5 minutes.

// Return the chicken to the pot. Add the soy sauce and cook for another 5 minutes. If you're going to make it spicy, add cayenne pepper now, starting with ½ teaspoon.

// Add the rice, the remaining tablespoon of salt, and the white pepper and stir to combine with the aromatics and chicken. Turn the heat up to high and add the chicken broth and/or water. Stir to make sure no rice is sticking to the bottom of the pot, and bring to a boil. Reduce the heat, stir again, and simmer for 30 minutes, loosely covered.

// Check the rice for doneness (if you're using brown rice, check in about 40 minutes); it should be soft, plump, and creamy. Turn off the heat once the rice is cooked. Grate in the fresh turmeric, if using. Fish out the chicken pieces, and when they are cool enough to handle, tear or chop the meat into bite-size pieces, discarding bones and skin. Stir the chicken back through the soup. Season with salt and cayenne pepper, as desired.

FOR DELIVERY

Include one quarter of the Last-Minute Greens, scallions, and cilantro.

TO SERVE

Reheat the soup, thinning with some broth or water if necessary (it will thicken considerably overnight). Add the Last-Minute Greens and stir them through. They will wilt almost at once. Ladle soup into bowls, add chopped scallions and cilantro, and drizzle with sesame oil and/or Sriracha.

WHY NOT DOUBLE IT?

// JULIE

On cool fall days in Indiana, my family spent Saturdays in the yard, raking leaves into piles for my dad to burn or for the four of us to jump into. Our welcome lunch break often involved my mom's beef chili, heavy with kidney beans and rich with the tomatoes she had canned from summer's bounty. Served with saltines and slices of cheddar, it was a dish I ate for the sustenance but also for the love.

My mom seemed to live in the kitchen, making three meals a day for her family, and I loved to be near as she assembled trays of lasagna, baked loaves of banana bread, and stirred pots of soup. Almost as often as these nourishing foods were for us, they were given to others: a friend with a new baby, the family down the street, a church gathering. *Why not double it?* seemed to be her mantra, learned perhaps from her own cooking mentor, my great-grandmother, who taught her that the joy of cooking lies in the sharing. More efficient than epicurean, my mom made food from scratch that served a function, and though gourmet was not a goal, she taught me that simple healthy food, cooked with love, results in happiness.

Summer visits to the nearby Amish farm and seasonal trips to pick-your-own orchards inspired in me an early appreciation of local and seasonal cooking. Pounds of tomatoes and buckets of peaches meant it was time to can for the winter; bushels of apples signaled that our freezer would soon be full of applesauce; heaps of berries promised fresh preserves and fruit-filled pancakes on gray February days. The unassuming symmetry of these colorful jars lined up on a basement shelf taught me that food could provide beauty as well as nourishment.

My interest in food and beauty took form in high school when I discovered my great-aunt's *Gourmet* magazines and received *Beyond Parsley*, a Junior League cookbook, as a graduation gift. I pored over the glossy pages and entertained my family and friends with food that seemed exotic by Midwestern standards: Herbed Stuffed Mushroom Caps and Zucchini Frittata, Brie wrapped in puff pastry, and Swiss Braided Bread. My mom seemed thrilled to be gaining an apprentice of sorts, and when I added my interest in nutrition, her cooking also began to evolve. The beef chili, for instance, was almost totally abandoned in favor of the new family favorite, what we now call Beck Chicken Chili.

When I moved to New York to study yoga, I worried that the urban environment would make fresh food and friendly community hard to find, but not only did I meet my husband and start a family fairly soon after, I also discovered kale on nearly every corner. And now, to my delight, becoming friends with Caroline, Tina, and Courtney and forming Soup Club has inspired me to invent new ways to cook and share healthful food that is both nourishing and flavorful.

When my family and I savor the soup that one of the Soup Club cooks has crafted, I am grateful to be continuing a story—one that began in other kitchens, long before any of us were born, where recipes were passed down through generations and meals stretched to feed as many as could fit around a table. Doubling the recipe is a standard I now live by. As I learned from my mom, it's nice to have the extra food, but it's even nicer to share it.

2 3-pound **chickens** (6 cups shredded, cooked chicken or, to speed things up, rotisserie chickens work just fine, too)

¼ cup **olive oil**

6 **garlic cloves**, minced

4 medium **yellow onions**, chopped

2 **red bell peppers**, cored, seeded, and chopped

2 **green bell peppers**, cored, seeded, and chopped

2 **jalapeño peppers**, seeded and minced

2 tablespoons **salt**, divided, plus more to taste

¼ cup plus 2 tablespoons **chili powder**

2 teaspoons ground **cumin**

2 teaspoons dried **oregano**

14 cups cooked **kidney beans** (from 2 pounds dried), cooking liquid reserved (see About Beans, page 21), or 8 15-ounce cans kidney beans, drained and rinsed

2 cups **tomato juice** (if using canned beans instead of dried)

2 cups chopped fresh **flat-leaf parsley**

1 cup chopped fresh **cilantro**

2 28-ounce cans diced **tomatoes**, with their juice

Freshly ground **black pepper**

2 bunches **scallions**, thinly sliced

Herbed Queso Fresco (page 46)

1 16-ounce bag **tortilla chips** (I like blue corn)

4 **avocados**

ANTS ON A LOG (page 229) is the traditional Beck accompaniment with this chili.

Clipped from an Orange County, California, newspaper by my Aunt Liz and mailed to my mom twenty-five years ago, chicken chili has been a family favorite ever since. It has made its way to my siblings' houses all over the country at some point: New York for fuel during fall break, Colorado for something warm and easy over the holidays, and Michigan for an impromptu early spring lunch. We make fun of my brother Kevin for his inclination to turn any leftover into a burrito. But these leftovers really do work wrapped in a tortilla, and so Kevin, enjoy without mockery. // JULIE

BECK CHICKEN CHILI

MAKES 8 QUARTS

Preheat the oven to 450°F.

// Place the chickens on a large roasting pan and roast for 50 to 60 minutes, until the juices run clear. Let cool and remove the skin and bones. Shred the chicken and set aside. (May be made up to 2 days in advance.)

// Heat the oil in the stockpot and add the garlic, onions, bell and jalapeño peppers, and 1 tablespoon of the salt. Sauté until the vegetables are soft, about 7 minutes. Add the chili powder, cumin, and oregano and cook for another 2 to 3 minutes.

// Add the beans plus 6 cups of reserved bean liquid to the onion mixture. If using canned beans, add 4 cups water and 2 cups tomato juice for a total of 6 cups liquid. Stir in the parsley, cilantro, diced tomatoes, and the remaining tablespoon of salt and bring to a boil. Reduce the heat and simmer for an hour, loosely covered, stirring occasionally to prevent sticking. Add more reserved bean liquid or water if the mixture becomes too dry.

// Add the shredded chicken and simmer for 5 more minutes. Season with salt and pepper.

FOR DELIVERY	**TO SERVE**
Include one quarter of the scallions, avocados, queso fresco, and tortilla chips.	Reheat the soup and serve topped with scallions, diced avocado, queso, and chips.

On cold winter days when I'm at work and have neglected to bring my lunch, I frequent a small takeout stand across from City Hall called Taqueria Nixtamalito. The Chicken Tortilla Soup is spicy and flavorful, loaded with chunks of chicken, veggies, and creamy avocado. I have been known to make a mad dash there even on the rainiest, coldest days. This recipe is my take, the beans my own addition to bulk up the soup and make it an even heartier meal. // COURTNEY

CHICKEN TORTILLA SOUP

MAKES 8 QUARTS

Preheat the oven to 350°F.

// Arrange the chicken on two large foil-lined rimmed baking sheets. Drizzle with 2 tablespoons of the olive oil and liberally sprinkle with salt and pepper. Roast for 20 to 25 minutes, or until cooked through. Set aside to cool. Once the chicken is cool, remove the skin and shred with two forks or break roughly into small pieces by hand. Set aside.

// Heat the remaining 4 tablespoons of oil in the stockpot and sauté the onions for about 7 minutes, until soft. Stir in the cumin, chili powder, and red pepper flakes, and cook for 5 minutes, until aromatic.

// Add the garlic, bell peppers, and carrots and stir to combine. Cook until the carrots begin to soften, about 15 minutes. Add the tomato paste and chicken, and stir to coat.

// Add the broth, beans, tomatoes with their juice, and bay leaves. Cover and bring to a boil. Reduce the heat to a simmer and continue to cook for 15 more minutes. Remove the bay leaves. Season with salt and pepper.

4 pounds boneless **chicken thighs** or **breasts**

6 tablespoons **olive oil**

5 teaspoons **salt**, plus more to taste

Freshly ground **black pepper**

6 medium **yellow onions**, diced

2 tablespoons ground **cumin**

1 tablespoon **chili powder**

1 teaspoon **red pepper flakes**, or to taste

1 head of **garlic** (about 10 cloves), minced

3 bell **pepper**s (yellow and red), cored, seeded, and diced

10 **carrots**, cut in ½-inch rounds

4 tablespoons **tomato paste**

4 quarts **chicken broth**

10 cups cooked **black beans** (from about 1½ pounds dried) or 5 15.5-ounce cans black beans, drained and rinsed

1 28-ounce can diced **tomatoes**, with their juice

3 **bay leaves**

3 dozen small **corn tortillas**

8 ounces **cotija cheese**

1 bunch **cilantro**

4 **avocados**

4 **limes**

FOR DELIVERY

Include one quarter of the tortillas, cheese, cilantro, avocado, and limes.

TO SERVE

Reheat the soup and portion in bowls. Slice the tortillas into strips and divide among the bowls. Top with crumbled cheese, diced avocado, a squeeze of lime, and cilantro leaves.

Giving a recipe for chicken soup sort of feels like telling someone else how to prepare their cereal and milk: The instructions are simple and intuitive but also loaded with infinite personal variables. My carrots are cut into circles; you may like short sticks. I finish with fresh parsley, but many recipes call for dill. One approach is to start with your own homemade Chicken Broth (page 30), adding cooked vegetables, noodles, and meat to the pot as it reheats—a Soup of Assembly. But making this soup from scratch is almost as easy, so here is one recipe, from which I assume everyone will deviate. // CAROLINE

JEWISH CHICKEN NOODLE SOUP

MAKES 8 QUARTS

If you are including matzo balls, prepare the dough and refrigerate (recipe follows).

// Heat the oil in the stockpot; add the carrots, onions, garlic, and celery; salt generously; and cook for 10 minutes, stirring occasionally.

// While the vegetables cook, bring two more pots of water to a boil, one for the matzo balls and one for the noodles.

// To the vegetable pot, add the chicken thighs and wings, 1 tablespoon of the salt, the Parmesan rind if using, and 8 quarts cold water (making sure the water covers the contents of the pot). Bring to a boil, reduce the heat, and simmer, loosely covered, for 30 minutes. Skim off any foam that rises to the top.

// While the soup is simmering, finish making the matzo balls (see page 136 for rolling and boiling instructions). Cook the noodles according to package directions, drain, toss them with a little oil to prevent sticking, and set aside.

// When the chicken thighs and wings are cooked all the way through (give them a poke to check), remove them from the pot and turn off the heat. Let the chicken cool a bit, then shred or chop the meat into bite-size pieces, discarding skin and bones.

// Fish out the onions, garlic, and large celery pieces and discard. Return the chicken meat to the pot. Season with salt and with pepper.

// recipe continues

Matzo Balls (optional, recipe follows)

3 tablespoons **olive oil**

1 pound **carrots**, cut into medium rounds

2 medium **yellow onions**, peeled and quartered

2 **garlic cloves**, peeled and lightly smashed

8 **celery stalks**, roughly chopped

1 tablespoon **salt**, plus more to taste

2½ pounds boneless, skinless **chicken thighs**

1 pound **chicken wings**

1 small piece of **Parmesan rind** (optional)

1 pound medium **egg noodles**; **angel hair pasta**, broken into small shards; or **small pasta**, such as ditalini

Freshly ground **black pepper**

1 bunch **flat-leaf parsley**, chopped

FOR DELIVERY

Include one quarter of the noodles, cooked matzo balls, and parsley or dill.

TO SERVE

Reheat the soup, matzo balls, and noodles separately. Add 2 small matzo balls to each bowl, add a small scoop of noodles, then ladle in the soup, making sure to get equal amounts of chicken and carrots all around. Top with parsley.

Matzo Balls

MAKES 48 SMALL MATZO BALLS

1 cup **matzo meal**

4 **eggs**, lightly beaten

2 tablespoons **schmaltz** or **vegetable oil**

2 teaspoons **seasoned salt**, or to taste

A pinch of ground **white pepper**

MATZO BALL COMMANDMENTS

Thou shalt try very hard to **ACQUIRE SOME SCHMALTZ**. Ironically, this dense fat (from a chicken, goose, or duck) yields the lightest matzo balls.

Thou shalt **KEEP THE POT COVERED** while the matzo balls are cooking, otherwise they get dense and you've wasted your good schmaltz.

Combine the matzo meal, eggs, schmaltz, seasoned salt, and white pepper in a medium mixing bowl and refrigerate for 20 minutes.

// Bring a large pot of water to a boil. Wet your hands, and form the dough into tablespoon-size balls, lining them up on a plate or rimmed baking sheet as you work.

// When all the matzo balls are ready, drop them into the boiling water, cover the pot (NO PEEKING!), reduce the heat, and simmer for 25 minutes. You may need to do this in batches.

// If not using immediately, let the matzo balls cool in their cooking liquid. Remove with a slotted spoon (discard the cooking liquid) and store DRY, in a sealed container, for up to 3 days in the refrigerator. Reheat by dropping the balls directly into boiling salted water. Why reheat separate from the chicken soup? Pure aesthetics: The matzo balls give off a lot of starch and will turn your golden broth cloudy. Matzo balls also freeze well in a zipper bag.

I am the one who takes two-gallon zipper bags to Thanksgiving dinner so that I can bring home the turkey carcass at the end of the night. I am also the one who, when hosting, follows my mother's example, always making a "four-legged" bird, roasting an extra set of drumsticks in the pan. Either way, I know I can make turkey soup over the holiday weekend. Let's assume that on Friday everyone eats turkey sandwiches all day, and Saturday is when the holiday parties happen. On Sunday, then, start the soup going sometime after your coffee and morning pie. Have it for an early dinner that night and put Thanksgiving to bed until next year. Or, for my Christmas-ham–inclined friends, make it with a leftover hambone instead of turkey. // *CAROLINE*

POST-THANKSGIVING TURKEY AND WHITE BEAN SOUP

MAKES 8 QUARTS

Start a quick soak of the beans (see About Beans, page 21), and while they soak, heat the oil in the stockpot and sauté the onions, celery, and carrots until soft, about 5 minutes. Add the turkey carcass, bay leaves, and salt and cover with about 5 quarts cold water. Bring to a boil, reduce the heat, and simmer gently, loosely covered, for 2 hours, stirring occasionally.

// Remove the turkey bones from the stockpot, and let sit on a plate or cutting board until cool enough to handle. Pull as much turkey meat off the bones as you can, and set aside. Discard the bones.

// Drain the soaked beans and rinse well in cold water, then add to the stockpot. Add the herb bundle and bring the soup back to a simmer for 45 minutes, loosely covered. Check the white beans for doneness, and continue to simmer until they're easy to bite into. (If using canned beans, let them simmer for 20 minutes before proceeding to the next step.)

// Remove the herb bundle and the bay leaves. Add the soup greens and cooked turkey meat. Stir well to submerge the greens, and loosely cover the pot. Continue to simmer until the greens are fully wilted, 5 to 10 minutes, depending on the greens. Season with salt and black pepper.

1 pound dried **white beans** (or use 4 15-ounce cans of white beans, drained and rinsed)

2 tablespoons **olive oil**

4 medium **yellow onions**, finely chopped

6 **celery stalks**, finely chopped

6 **carrots**, chopped into medium rounds

1 leftover **turkey carcass**, plus any leftover turkey meat you want to use up, or 2 to 3 pounds raw turkey wings, thighs, and/or necks, skin removed

2 **bay leaves**

1 tablespoon **salt**, plus more to taste

2 sprigs each **flat-leaf parsley**, **rosemary**, and **thyme**, tied together with kitchen twine

3 large bunches **winter greens**, such as collards, escarole, and kale, thick ribs removed, leaves finely sliced

Freshly ground **black pepper**

1 bunch **flat-leaf parsley**, chopped

FOR DELIVERY

Include one quarter of the chopped parsley, and any Thanksgiving leftovers you want to share: Corn Casserole (page 187), Marinated Brussels Sprouts (page 171), Black Olive Shortbread (page 191), or Red Cabbage Salad (page 161).

FOR SERVING

Top with chopped fresh parsley and red pepper flakes.

6 tablespoons (¾ stick) **butter**

2½ pounds **andouille sausage**, pricked with a fork on all sides

1½ pounds boneless, skinless **chicken thighs**, 7 or 8 total

Salt and freshly ground **black pepper**

Vegetable oil, if needed, for the roux

¾ cup **all-purpose flour**

6 medium **yellow onions**, thickly sliced

6 **celery stalks**, chopped

3 large **green bell peppers**, cored, seeded, and chopped

6 **garlic cloves**, minced

3 pounds **okra**, trimmed and cut into thirds (approximately 1-inch pieces)

2 28-ounce cans chopped **tomatoes**, with their juice

3 quarts **chicken broth**

2 large bunches **collard greens**, thinly sliced

12 sprigs **thyme**, leaves only

4 **bay leaves**

8 cups cooked **white rice**

1 large bunch **flat-leaf parsley**, chopped

8 **scallions**, chopped

Filé powder (see Note)

———————

FILÉ (pronounce "fee-lay") is made from ground sassafras root. It gives gumbo its distinctive flavor and also acts as a slight thickener when used in cooking. If you can't find it in your grocery's spice section, you can order a small tin online to divide among your Soup Club.

Why am I entering the gumbo fray? This is a hallowed dish of New Orleans, a city in which I have spent a total of six days, five and a half of those hunched over a computer on a job, picking at muffuletta scraps. I will give credit to my meat-loving hometown, Chicago, whose residents welcome the opportunity to combine different proteins in one dish (including my mother, who made gumbo regularly in the winter).

There are as many rules for gumbo as there are cooks who make it. The roux and the okra, my two non-negotiables, are redundant or optional for others with a far more authentic claim to know. As my friend Bob, a true worshipper of the city, informed me with confidence, "The roux should be coffee-colored." (I had, in my naïveté, been stopping at iced tea.) // CAROLINE

CHICKEN, ANDOUILLE, AND OKRA GUMBO

MAKES 8 QUARTS

Melt 4 tablespoons of the butter in the stockpot. In batches, brown the sausages on both sides, 1 to 2 minutes per side, then remove to a plate. Sprinkle the chicken thighs with salt and pepper on both sides and brown in the same pot, 1 to 2 minutes per side. When the sausages and chicken are cool, cut into bite-size chunks.

// Make the roux, which calls for equal amounts fat and flour. Eyeball the rendered fat in the bottom of the pot, which should measure about ¾ cup. Add vegetable oil if needed. Heat the fat, add the flour, and cook over medium heat, stirring constantly, until the mixture is coffee colored and aromatic, about 15 minutes. Add the onions, celery, green peppers, and garlic and sauté until softened, about 10 minutes.

// While the vegetables cook, melt the remaining 2 tablespoons butter in a large skillet and brown the okra in batches, turning once or twice. Add the okra, sausage, and chicken back to the stockpot, along with any juices that have collected.

// Add the tomatoes and their juice, the broth, collards, thyme, bay leaves, and 3 teaspoons salt. Bring to a boil, reduce the heat, and simmer until slightly thickened, making sure not to overcook or the okra will get slimy, 25 to 30 minutes. Discard the bay leaves. Season with salt and pepper.

FOR DELIVERY

Include one quarter of the rice, parsley, and scallions. Check for your Soup Club mates' stock of filé powder; very little is required for the gumbo, but I think it's necessary.

TO SERVE

Reheat the gumbo, and serve over white rice. Top with parsley and scallions and a pinch of filé powder.

3 tablespoons **olive oil**

2½ pounds **ground beef**

8 medium **yellow onions**, sliced thin

1 head of **garlic** (about 10 cloves), minced

4½ teaspoons ground **cumin**

4½ teaspoons ground **coriander**

4½ teaspoons dried **oregano**

2½ teaspoons **chili powder**

4 28-ounce cans crushed **tomatoes**, with
their juice

1 quart **chicken broth** or beef broth

1 pound dried **black beans**, soaked
(see About Beans, page 21), or
10 cups cooked or canned beans,
drained and rinsed

2 **cinnamon** sticks

⅔ cup **espresso powder**

5 ounces **unsweetened chocolate**, roughly
chopped

1 tablespoon **salt**, plus more to taste

Freshly ground **black pepper**

8 **scallions** (green parts only), chopped

1 bunch **cilantro**, minced

1 cup **sour cream**

1 full recipe **Cheddar Cornbread** (page 183)

4 2-5 ounce **dark chocolate bars**
(70% or higher cocoa content)

When I was a child we always had a simple beef and bean chili on Christmas Eve. In an effort to be helpful to my grandmother, who took great pride in the Christmas preparations she made for the family, my grandfather (Papa)—not the best decorator—took it upon himself to make chili for everyone to eat before they trimmed the tree. My grandparents are no longer with us, but each year my mother still makes chili on Christmas Eve. In recent years she has been open to interpretation. Here's to new traditions! // COURTNEY

BEEF MOLE CHILI

MAKES 8 QUARTS

Heat the oil in the stockpot. Brown the ground beef in batches (do not crowd the pan). Remove the meat with a slotted spoon, set aside on a plate, and discard the extra grease as you go, leaving just enough to coat the pan.

// Add the onions and sauté until softened, about 7 minutes.

// Add the garlic and sauté for an additional 2 minutes, reducing the heat as needed to prevent the onions and garlic from browning. Stir in the cumin, coriander, oregano, and chili powder until combined, scraping the bottom of the pan with a spatula and removing from the heat once the mixture is fragrant.

// Add the tomatoes and their juice. Stir well to combine, and bring to a boil. Add the broth, beans, cinnamon sticks, espresso, and chocolate. Stir to combine and simmer for 30 minutes, loosely covered, stirring occasionally to prevent sticking. Add water if the mixture becomes too dry. Add the ground beef and 1 tablespoon of the salt. Stir well and simmer for at least 30 minutes more, covered, over low heat. Remove the cinnamon sticks. Season with salt and pepper.

FOR DELIVERY
Include one quarter of the chopped scallions, minced cilantro, sour cream, and cornbread and 1 chocolate bar.

TO SERVE
Reheat and top with sour cream, scallions, cilantro, and crumbled cornbread. Grate additional chocolate on top.

// *recipe continues*

Papa's Chili

MAKES 8 QUARTS

3 tablespoons **vegetable** or **canola oil**

4 medium **yellow onions**, diced

4 pounds **ground beef**

4 teaspoons **salt**

4 14½-ounce cans diced **tomatoes** with their juice

1 6-ounce can **tomato paste**

1 pound dried **kidney beans**, soaked (see About Beans, page 21), or 10 cups cooked or canned beans, drained and rinsed

4 tablespoons **chili powder**, plus more to taste

4 **garlic cloves**, smashed

Heat the oil in the stockpot. Add the onions and sauté until translucent, 7 to 10 minutes. Brown the ground beef with the onions in batches, being careful not to steam. Add all the beef back to the pot and stir in the salt, tomatoes, tomato paste, beans (soaked but not cooked), chili powder, and garlic. Add water if needed to loosen. Bring to a simmer and cook, partially covered, for 2 hours. If using canned beans, add after 1 hour. Serve atop saltine crackers.

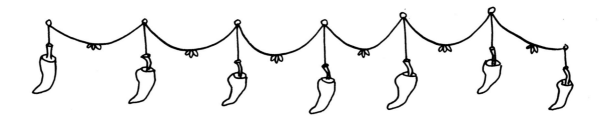

Cooking in Quantity

We talked to some experts: Our local firefighters. When they're not out on life-threatening and life-saving calls, all thirteen of them cook and eat together at the firehouse. We spoke with Dan, who learned to cook there. Here are some tips he's picked up over the years.

- Cooking in the firehouse is very democratic—you work your way up from dishwasher—and cooks take turns (just like Soup Club!).

- One of the guys is a two-time chili cookoff champion. His trick is to add a bottle of Dr. Pepper and use 80/20 ground beef. Always serve with cornbread on the side.

- Ratios, rather than recipes, guide their cooking. For example, Dan uses 2 cans of tomatoes per pound of meat (for bolognese, chili, etc.).

- They take the fire truck to the grocery store and don't shop with a recipe in mind. The meal is built around a protein, and the protein of choice is whatever's on sale.

- Dan's creole gumbo starts with a roux that he cooks to "Brick Red . . . really, as dark as you can." (For comparison, see page 138.)

- When it isn't soup or chili, our firehouse loves a big tray of "Knotty Chops"—pork chops marinated in pickled peppers and baked. (See page 200 for more Big Food to share.)

- Firefighters do not use cookbooks, but Dan promises to test out some Soup Club favorites and report back.

2 pounds dried **chorizo sausage**, sliced into ⅛-inch rounds (optional)

1½ cups **olive oil**, plus more if needed

4 medium **yellow onions**, chopped

1 head of **garlic** (about 10 cloves), chopped

6 pounds **russet potatoes**, scrubbed, peeled, and chopped

3 tablespoons **salt**, plus more to taste

4 large bunches **kale** (about 40 ounces), stems trimmed and cut into a very fine julienne

Freshly ground **black pepper**

4 small **whole-wheat boules**

" **COURTNEY:** Shortly after our son was born he was hospitalized with a severe virus. That led to intubation and a ventilator, to feeding tubes and chest X-rays. Upon hearing we were living in the hospital, Caroline set up a food delivery schedule among our friends that sustained us nightly whether we were eating in the hospital or with our two-year-old at home. It was before we discovered glass jars and before any of us thought about or talked about Soup Club. Home-cooked meals, ready to eat or reheat, were delivered to our door until after we were home from the hospital nearly six weeks later. The first time I tasted Julie's Caldo Verde it was reheated in a paper bowl in the microwave of the Beth Israel Hospital pediatric ICU. It was the best soup I had ever tasted. To this day we refer to it as "the hospital soup" and it is revered at our house.

My husband, Rusty, taught me how to make this soup early on in our relationship, and whenever it's simmering on the stove, I am reminded of those first sweet months of being together. He learned it during medical school from his next-door neighbor, who told him to "take equal weights kale and potatoes, a quarter that of olive oil, maybe some chorizo, cover with water, and cook." It inspired Rusty's visit to a restaurant supply store that yielded the fourteen-quart stockpot that's now the foundation of our household's soup-making enterprise twenty years later. We've worked on the formula over the years, but the art of this soup is in how you cut the kale: The thinner and more consistently you slice it, the more refined the texture—a nearly surgical task I often leave to my competent sous-chef. // JULIE

CALDO VERDE

MAKES 8 QUARTS

Working in batches, brown the sliced chorizo on both sides in the stockpot. Add a tablespoon of olive oil if it sticks. Remove the sausage from the pot and set aside.

// Heat 1 cup of the olive oil in the stockpot and sauté the onions and garlic until soft, about 7 minutes. Scrape the bottom of the pot a bit while sautéing in order to get the browned sausage bits to mix into the onion mixture.

// Add the potatoes and sauté for 3 minutes. Add 4 quarts of cold water and bring to a boil. Reduce the heat, add the salt, and simmer for 25 to 30 minutes, or until the potatoes are soft. Remove from the heat and briefly puree the soup with an immersion blender, about 10 seconds. You are not looking for a silky smooth consistency here.

// Add the kale and the remaining ½ cup of the olive oil and stir until mixed. Season with salt and pepper.

FOR DELIVERY	TO SERVE
Include one quarter of the prepared chorizo and 1 boule.	Reheat the soup along with the chorizo and stir in a glug of olive oil, if desired. Cut the hearty boule into generous chunks and serve warm with the soup.

In 1990, I offered my soon-to-be friend Rob Viola a ride as he was walking on the side of the road making his way home from high school. I drove a penny-colored diesel Rabbit. He sported a mop of nearly shoulder-length curls. He did not mock my Grateful Dead bumper sticker. Soon I was doing my homework in his kitchen, while his dad cooked and Rob's band practiced downstairs. Our friendship lasted through high school shenanigans, college visits, a shared house in Philadelphia, and a synchronous migration to New York. Rob's dad cooked a lot for the family, but the dish Rob raved most about through the years was this Italian Wedding Soup, a Christmas Day staple for his large Italian family. Now, more than twenty years later, Rob and I are still friends (and so are our kids and spouses), and he has finally shared this family recipe with me. // COURTNEY

ITALIAN WEDDING SOUP

MAKES 8 QUARTS

In the stockpot, bring the broth to a boil, reduce the heat, and simmer while you make the meatballs.

// Combine the parsley, egg, salt, garlic, and bread crumbs in a medium bowl, stirring with a fork to combine. Mix in the ground meat and ½ cup plus 2 tablespoons of the cheese. Form into tightly packed small balls no bigger than 1 teaspoon. (They need to be tightly packed so they don't fall apart in the soup.)

// Gently add the meatballs to the broth, along with the escarole and the Parmesan rinds. Lower the heat and simmer, covered, for 2 hours minimum and up to 4 hours if possible. Discard the Parmesan rinds. Season with salt and pepper.

6½ quarts **Chicken Broth** (page 30)

1 bunch **flat-leaf parsley**, chopped

1 **egg**

1 teaspoon **salt**, plus more to taste

6 **garlic cloves**, minced

½ cup plus 2 tablespoons **seasoned bread crumbs** (such as Progresso seasoned bread crumbs)

½ pound **ground beef**

½ pound **ground pork**

½ pound **ground veal**

12 ounces **Pecorino Romano cheese**, grated (2 cups)

1 large head **escarole**, coarsely chopped

4 large pieces **Parmesan rind**

Freshly ground **black pepper**

4 small loaves **crusty bread** (such as ciabatta)

FOR DELIVERY

Include one quarter of the remaining cheese and 1 loaf of bread. Before you make your delivery, check that your Soup Mates have eggs on hand. They'll need two eggs per quart of soup.

TO SERVE

Reheat the soup and, just before serving, beat 2 eggs per quart in a liquid measuring cup. Remove the soup from the heat and stir briskly in a circular motion. Slowly pour the eggs into the swirling soup to form long delicate ribbons. Serve with bread and Pecorino on top.

" **ROB SAYS:** "If you have kids available for meatball rolling their tiny hands make great tiny meatballs."

PART THREE

FOOD FOR FORKS & FINGERS

And now, after making our case for Soup, Soup, Soup, it's time to share our dirty little secret: Soup Club isn't always about soup.

Sometimes you want to make a Winter Caesar Salad (page 158) at home to eat with your soup delivery. Some soups get delivered with a side dish like Green Beans with Mustard and Almonds (page 165). Sometimes you're having a dinner party or going to a potluck, and you want to make a Zucchini and Sun-Dried Tomato Lasagna (page 209). Or you need roasted vegetables on the table to make your leftover soup a full meal (see page 169). Once in a while, you get really excited about perfect Squash Bread (page 184). Hence this whole big selection of recipes that we like to call Food for Forks and Fingers.

SALADS & DRESSINGS

We love salad, on its own and as a refreshing
counterpoint to our soups. Although salads can be made
without a recipe, we do have some favorite dressings
and combinations of leafy greens and their vegetable
companions. Like our soups, these salad recipes feed a
crowd, so feel free to halve the amounts as needed, or why
not just make the full amount and share freely?

A FEW NOTES ABOUT SALAD DRESSING

- There are salad makers out there who dress their salads intuitively, right into the bowl: a little oil, some salt, a spritz of lemon, more oil, other spices and herbs. We applaud that skill, and we also acknowledge that it's not universal.

- Essential Tool: One clean pint-size glass jar with a tight-fitting lid (recycled peanut butter jars are great for this). Secure a strip of paper towel around the lid with a rubber band to catch any drips from shaking and pouring.

- Making a garlic paste is a useful way to distribute garlic flavor throughout a dressing. Smash the garlic on a cutting board, remove the peel, and cover the garlic with salt. Using the flat side of a large knife, press and scrape the garlic back and forth across the board until it forms a paste. Courtney calls this spackling.

LEMON-SHALLOT VINAIGRETTE

MAKES 2 CUPS

Allow the garlic and shallots to macerate for a few minutes to mellow their sharpness. Use with Greek Orzo (page 194) and Bean Salad with Pickled Vegetables (page 159).
// TINA AND COURTNEY

> 4 **garlic** cloves
>
> 2 teaspoons **salt**
>
> 1 small **shallot**, minced (about ¼ cup)
>
> Grated zest of 2 **lemons**
>
> ½ cup freshly squeezed **lemon juice** (from 3 to 4 lemons)
>
> ¼ cup **cider vinegar** or champagne vinegar
>
> 1 teaspoon finely ground **black pepper**
>
> 1 cup plus 2 tablespoons **olive oil**

Combine the garlic and salt together to make a paste. Place the paste into a glass jar with a tight-fitting lid and add the shallot, lemon zest and juice, vinegar, and pepper. Stir to combine and set aside for 10 minutes.

// Whisk in the oil or pour the oil in, cap the jar, and shake vigorously so the ingredients emulsify.

WALNUT VINAIGRETTE

MAKES 2 CUPS

The order of operations for this dressing came from the host of a dinner party I went to, when I was just out of college. She said it had been handed down through the generations from her husband's family. I received it as gospel and haven't deviated from the formula since. Use it over Kale and Mustard Greens (page 163), roasted vegetables (see page 169), and Marinated Brussels Sprouts (page 171).
// CAROLINE

> 2 teaspoons **salt**
>
> 1 teaspoon freshly ground **black pepper**
>
> 2 teaspoons **Dijon mustard**
>
> 6 ounces **sherry vinegar**
>
> 1 **garlic** clove, smashed
>
> 6 ounces **olive oil**
>
> 3 ounces **walnut oil**

In a glass jar with a tight-fitting lid, combine the salt and pepper. Add the Dijon mustard and mix to a grainy paste. Pour in the vinegar and whisk to combine. Add the garlic clove and oils. Cap the jar and shake vigorously to emulsify, and always re-shake before using.

NOTE: *Experiment with the proportion of mustard to oil to vinegar. I like it quite vinegary, which works well on salads with sturdier greens, beans, and grains.*

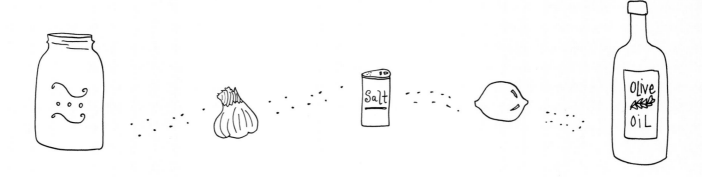

LIME DRESSING

MAKES 2 CUPS

Use this for Tomato-Watermelon Salad (page 155) or Corn and Red Pepper Salad (page 159). It is also good over chopped avocados sprinkled with coarse sea salt. // TINA AND JULIE

1 **garlic** clove
2 teaspoons **salt**
1 cup freshly squeezed **lime juice** (from 12 to 16 limes)
1 cup **olive oil**

Make a paste with the garlic and salt. Transfer to a glass jar with a tight-fitting lid, add the lime juice and oil, cap the jar, and shake vigorously so the ingredients emulsify.

SOY-SESAME DRESSING

MAKES 2 CUPS

This is great for any of the Cucumber Salad Variations (page 155). Also, try it with the Pan-Asian Cabbage Salad (page 161). // COURTNEY

½ cup **soy sauce**
1 cup **unseasoned rice vinegar** (or white wine vinegar)
¼ cup **sugar**
⅓ cup **sesame oil**

Add the soy sauce, vinegar, sugar, and oil to a jar with a tight-fitting lid. Cap the jar and shake well to combine.

LEMON DRESSING

MAKES 2 CUPS

Delicious on the Butter Lettuce and Radish Salad (page 156) and Red Cabbage Salad (page 161). // JULIE

1 **garlic** clove
2 teaspoons **salt**
⅔ cup freshly squeezed **lemon juice** (from 3 to 4 lemons)
1⅓ cups **olive oil**
½ teaspoon freshly ground **black pepper**

Make a paste with the garlic and salt. Combine with the lemon juice, oil, and pepper in a glass jar with a tight-fitting lid. Cap the jar and shake well to combine.

BALSAMIC VINAIGRETTE

MAKES 2 CUPS

After eating salads with store-bought ranch dressing most of my young life, it was thrilling to taste greens dressed simply with oil and vinegar at a friend's house in high school. Kale and Mustard Greens (page 163) receive this vinaigrette well, as do chilled grain and pasta salads. // JULIE

1 **garlic** clove
2 teaspoons **salt**
⅓ cup **balsamic vinegar**
3 tablespoons **Dijon mustard**
1 teaspoon pure **maple syrup**
½ teaspoon freshly ground **black pepper**
1½ cups **olive oil**

Combine the garlic and salt together to make a paste. In a glass jar with a tight-fitting lid, mix together the garlic paste, vinegar, mustard, maple syrup, and pepper. Pour in the olive oil, cap the jar, and shake vigorously to combine.

CAESAR DRESSING OR AIOLI

MAKES ABOUT 1 CUP

This emulsion of egg yolk, garlic, and olive oil has two great endpoints: You can go the anchovy-Parmesan route and call it Caesar dressing, or you can omit the anchovies and add the extra garlic for an aioli dip. Either way, be slow, steady, and patient when adding the oil. // CAROLINE

- 2 **egg yolks** (save the whites for Sweet and Spicy Nuts, page 234)
- 1 or 2 **garlic cloves**, minced
- ¼ cup freshly squeezed **lemon juice** (from 1 to 2 lemons)
- 2 oil-packed **anchovy fillets**, minced (for Caesar Dressing)
- ¼ or ½ cup **olive oil** (also okay to mix this with a more flavorful oil, such as walnut, hazelnut, pumpkin seed)
- **Salt** and freshly ground **black pepper**
- ¼ cup grated **Parmigiano-Reggiano cheese** (for Caesar Dressing)

FOR CAESAR DRESSING: *Use 1 garlic clove, the anchovies, and ½ cup oil.*

FOR AIOLI: *Use 2 garlic cloves and ¼ cup oil and omit the anchovies.*

Whisk the egg yolks in a small bowl with the garlic and lemon juice. Add the anchovies, if using.

// Slowly add the olive oil, starting with a few drops at a time, whisking well to incorporate before adding more. Once about half the olive oil is used up and the mixture is emulsified, add the rest of the oil in a thin, steady stream. Keep whisking.

// Add several big grinds of pepper, then taste. Whisk in a little more lemon juice, salt, and pepper to taste. Stop here for aioli.

// For Caesar dressing, whisk in the cheese just before dressing the salad.

// Store in the refrigerator, in a tightly covered glass jar, for up to 4 days. For variations, whisk in 1 teaspoon Dijon mustard, 1 teaspoon curry powder, or 1 tablespoon minced herbs after all the oil.

2 eggs + OLive OiL + lemon
+ 2 garlic cloves = Aioli
+ 1 garlic clove + anchovy + parmesan = CAESAR

This salad is fun to take to picnics. It's best to toss the watermelon into the salad as late as possible, and no more than a couple hours before serving, so it maintains its melon integrity. Any fresh herb will complement the flavors, but cilantro is my favorite. // TINA

TOMATO-WATERMELON SALAD

SERVES 8 TO 10

2 quarts cherry **tomatoes**, quartered

2 quarts 1-inch **watermelon** cubes (from about ½ large watermelon)

¾ cup chopped fresh **cilantro**, **basil**, or **mint** leaves

¾ cup **Lime Dressing** (page 153, plus more to taste

4 **avocados**, halved, pitted, peeled, and cubed

2 cups cubed or crumbled **salty cheese**, such as **feta** or **cotija**

If serving immediately, toss the tomatoes, watermelon, and cilantro together with the dressing. Top with the avocado and cheese.

// If preparing in advance, toss the tomatoes with the dressing and top with the avocado and cheese. Chill the watermelon separately and toss it all together just before plating.

o o o o o o o o o o o o o o o o o

Sometimes I find myself bored with green salad but still craving a cold side to serve with soup. Cucumber salads are my ten-minute go-to that always feel fancier than they are. It's hard to go wrong with any of these as long as you follow a couple quick rules. If you are using a standard cucumber, peel it, halve it, and scoop out the seeds. If you are using an English (hothouse) cucumber, there is no need to peel or seed. // COURTNEY

CUCUMBER SALAD VARIATIONS

SERVES 8

CREAMY CUCUMBER SALAD

4 cucumbers

¼ cup **Greek yogurt**

½ teaspoon **salt**

2 tablespoons chopped fresh **dill** (dried dill doesn't work here)

SIMPLE VINEGAR CUCUMBER SALAD

4 cucumbers

1 small **white onion**, very thinly sliced

¼ cup **olive oil**

2 tablespoons **white vinegar** (white wine, champagne, or white balsamic also work)

4 to 6 **chives** or the green part of a scallion, sliced thin

SOY-SESAME CUCUMBER SALAD

4 cucumbers

Soy-Sesame Dressing (page 153)

Peel and halve the cucumbers lengthwise. Scoop out the seeds with a sharp spoon. Slice the cucumbers widthwise into crescents ¼ inch thick (salt and drain if preparing more than 30 minutes ahead).

// Dress the cucumbers to taste. Stir in the fresh herbs, reserving a large pinch to garnish the top of the salad before serving. Chill for 30 minutes before serving.

2 small heads **escarole** (1½ pounds total), torn into bite-size pieces

Lemon Dressing (page 153)

½ cup shaved or grated **Parmigiano-Reggiano cheese**

1 medium **grapefruit**, segmented, pith and peel removed, chopped into bite-size pieces

Salt and freshly ground **black pepper**

½ cup **hazelnuts**, skins removed, nuts chopped and toasted

Serve with any of the wintery pureed soups, like Roasted Winter Squash and Sweet Potato Soup (page 90), Chestnut Soup (page 78), or Sunchoke Soup (page 89).

Dirt really clings to escarole leaves, and you have to wash them well, rubbing the base of each leaf.

Escarole is a key green for both soups and salads. It's a bright, crisp member of the endive family and grows late into the cold months, making it perfect for winter salads. The addition of grapefruit makes it a refreshing palate cleanser and the hazelnuts lend a sweet crunch. // JULIE

ESCAROLE, GRAPEFRUIT, AND HAZELNUT SALAD

SERVES 8 TO 10

In a large bowl, toss the greens with enough of the lemon dressing to coat well. Add the cheese and toss to combine. Mix in the grapefruit pieces, a large pinch of salt, and some freshly ground pepper. Top with the hazelnuts and serve.

∘ ∘ ∘ ∘ ∘ ∘ ∘ ∘ ∘ ∘ ∘ ∘ ∘ ∘ ∘ ∘

1 **garlic** clove, sliced in half

4 heads **butter** lettuce (3 pounds), torn into bite-size pieces

Lemon Dressing (page 153)

10 **radishes**, thinly sliced

Salt and freshly ground **black pepper**

Never underestimate the power of a simple salad. If you can't find butter lettuce, any tender leafy lettuce will do here. // COURTNEY

BUTTER LETTUCE AND RADISH SALAD

SERVES 8 TO 10

Rub a large wooden salad bowl with the cut sides of the garlic clove. Add the lettuce and toss the greens with enough dressing to coat well. Portion on plates and scatter radish slices generously over the greens. Season with salt and pepper to taste.

1 head **radicchio**, cored and thinly sliced

1 large bunch **kale** (about 8 ounces), thick stems removed and thinly sliced

1 small head **escarole** or **frisée** or 2 heads endive, cored and thinly sliced

Olive oil

Salt and freshly ground **black pepper**

Caesar Dressing (page 154)

3 cups roasted **sweet potato** or **cauliflower** (see page 169), cut into bite-size pieces (optional)

2 **Bosc pears**, quartered, cored, and thinly sliced (tart, crisp apples can substitute)

1 cup chopped **walnuts** or **pecans**, toasted

¼ cup grated **Parmigiano-Reggiano cheese**

Caesar dressing is a great match for winter produce, which doesn't wilt under its creamy weight. If you feel architectural, style this salad as a DIY appetizer: Instead of slicing all the greens, just separate the leaves, keeping them whole, and arrange them on a wide, shallow dish. Or, arrange the tall leaves in some glass jars for a salad bouquet (my friend Noelle did this in college and I was dazzled). Either way, serve the dressing in the center with a couple of spoons, for people to dip into as they choose. // **CAROLINE**

WINTER CAESAR SALAD

SERVES 8 TO 10

Toss the greens together first. Drizzle them with a little olive oil, and season with a large pinch of salt and a few grindings of pepper. Toss to coat evenly.

// Add ¼ cup of the dressing, and toss again. Add the roasted vegetables, if using; half of the pears; ½ cup of the walnuts; and ¼ cup more dressing. Toss again, adding salt and pepper to taste.

// Add the remaining pears and walnuts on top of the salad, and sprinkle with the cheese.

Nothing shouts summer to me like corn on the cob. This salad has endless possibilities. Take or leave the black beans; roast, grill, or boil the corn; or increase the citrus and decrease the cilantro. The one piece that cannot change is buying farm-fresh corn and shucking it yourself. That's the best part. My kids beg for the opportunity. // JULIE

10 ears fresh **corn**, shucked

2 **red bell peppers**, cored, seeded, and diced

1 15-ounce can **black beans**, drained and rinsed

¾ cup fresh **cilantro** leaves, chopped

Lime Dressing (page 153)

Salt and freshly ground **black pepper**

2 **avocados**, halved, pitted, peeled, and diced (optional)

CORN AND RED PEPPER SALAD

SERVES 8 TO 10

Bring a large pot of water to a boil and add the ears of corn. Cook for 3 to 5 minutes, loosely covered, and then plunge the corn into ice water to set its color and doneness.

// Once the corn is cooled, cut the kernels off the cobs and put into a medium mixing bowl. Add the bell peppers, black beans, and cilantro and stir to combine.

// Toss the salad with about ½ cup of the Lime Dressing, adding more if desired. Season with salt and pepper. Top with avocado, if using, right before serving.

When Caroline's Quick Pickles (page 167) join this classic, something fantastic happens. If you are looking to bulk the bean salad up a bit, thinly shredded red cabbage adds color, more crunch, and fresh flavor. It's best when you start with dried beans (see page 21), but canned will work just fine. // TINA

8 cups assorted **cooked beans** (such as black beans, white beans, chickpeas, or kidney beans)

Lemon-Shallot Vinaigrette (page 152)

2 jars **Quick Pickles** (page 167) or 4 cups **pickled vegetables**, diced

8 **celery stalks**, finely sliced

2 to 6 cups thinly sliced **red cabbage** (optional)

Salt and freshly ground **black pepper**

BEAN SALAD WITH PICKLED VEGETABLES

SERVES 8 TO 10

Mix together the beans and ½ cup of the vinaigrette. Add the pickled vegetables, celery, and the red cabbage, if using, and mix well. Add more vinaigrette as needed and season with salt and pepper.

Red cabbage adds color and crunch to any salad, but it also works well on its own. Try substituting fennel for the red cabbage, or try the pan-Asian version below for a 1980s throwback. // JULIE

RED CABBAGE SALAD

SERVES 8 TO 10

1 large or 2 small heads **red cabbage** (3½ to 4 pounds total), shredded

6 to 8 **scallions**, finely chopped

1 bunch **flat-leaf parsley**, finely chopped

Lemon Dressing (page 153)

½ cup finely grated **Parmigiano-Reggiano** cheese

Salt and freshly ground **black pepper**

Pull away the outer leaves of the cabbage and discard any bruised leaves. Cut the cabbage in half and in half again through the core. Remove the tough white core and then begin to slice the cabbage into strips as fine as you can accomplish. Get really specific; if the strips are too thick, the cabbage won't absorb the dressing well.

// In a large salad bowl, toss together the cabbage, scallions, and parsley and mix with several spoonfuls of the lemon dressing. Stir or use your hands to coat the salad well. Add the cheese and more dressing as needed. Season with salt and pepper.

VARIATION

For Fennel Salad: *Omit the red cabbage and use 6 to 8 small fennel bulbs (3½ to 4 pounds), stems and outer leaves trimmed and discarded. Finely shred the fennel and follow the instructions above.*

Pan-Asian Cabbage Salad

Heat the butter in a small pan, and add the ramen, sesame seeds, and almonds. Mix to combine, then break up the noodles into small pieces and toast until golden. Remove from the heat and set aside.

// Combine the shredded cabbages, scallions, and toasted ramen mix in a large salad bowl and toss with several spoonfuls of the vinaigrette. Mix until well combined. Season with salt and pepper.

2 tablespoons **butter**

1 3-ounce package instant **ramen noodles** (discard seasoning pack), uncooked

½ cup **sesame seeds**

½ cup sliced **almonds**

1 small head **napa cabbage**, shredded

1 small head **red cabbage**, shredded

6 to 8 **scallions**, finely chopped

Soy-Sesame Dressing (page 153)

Salt and freshly ground **black pepper**

1 pound black **Beluga lentils** or French green **lentils** (about 2 cups)

2 to 4 cups **vegetable broth**

1 teaspoon **salt**, plus more to taste

1 small **butternut squash**, peeled and chopped into ½-inch cubes (about 4 cups)

½ tablespoon **olive oil**

Freshly ground **black pepper**

1 small **red onion**, thinly sliced

5 **celery stalks**, very finely sliced

Lemon-Shallot Vinaigrette (page 152)

2 bunches **flat-leaf parsley**, very finely chopped

1 cup **walnuts**, chopped and toasted (see Nuts and Seeds, page 50)

2 cups crumbled **goat** or **feta cheese**

This hearty salad is perfect alone or as an accompaniment to a Potato Tortilla (page 228) or fish. Beluga lentils or French green lentils (also known as Puy lentils) hold their shape when cooked—and when cooked with broth, they have an even deeper, richer flavor. This salad can be served immediately or after hanging out in the refrigerator for a couple of days. // TINA

LENTIL SQUASH SALAD

SERVES 8 TO 10

Preheat the oven to 400°F.

// Sort and rinse the lentils, place in a medium pot, then pour in a total of 4 cups of liquid, either all broth or a combination of broth and water. Bring to a boil, add ½ teaspoon of the salt, reduce to a simmer, and cook, uncovered, for about 20 minutes, until the lentils are just becoming tender.

// Meanwhile, spread the butternut squash cubes in a single layer on a foil-lined rimmed baking sheet. Drizzle with the oil and toss with your hands to evenly coat. Sprinkle with the remaining ½ teaspoon of salt and a few grinds of pepper. Roast for 25 to 30 minutes, or until tender and golden, tossing once or twice while in the oven.

// When the lentils are cooked al dente, remove them from the heat and pour off any liquid that has not cooked off. (Do not rinse the lentils in cold water to stop the cooking, since some of the flavor will also be washed away.) Uncover and stir to release the steam. Let them cool for 5 to 10 minutes.

// While still warm, toss the lentils with the roasted squash, red onion, celery, and ½ cup of the vinaigrette. Taste and add more dressing, salt, and pepper as needed. Mix in the parsley when the salad has cooled further.

// Top with the nuts and crumbled cheese before serving.

Kale has not only arrived, it has moved in and bought some property and is running for a seat on the community board. There's no one way to eat a kale salad, but it does pair really well with mustard greens. Unadorned, kale can be almost grassy, while mustard greens taste as spicy as Dijon; but there's some magic mellowing that happens when they get mixed and doused with salt, oil, and vinegar. // JULIE & CAROLINE

1 bunch **lacinato kale** (12 ounces), stems removed and cut into small pieces

1 bunch **mustard greens** (12 ounces), cut into small pieces

½ cup **pepitas** (raw green pumpkin seeds), toasted

Balsamic Vinaigrette (page 153) or **Walnut Vinaigrette** (page 152)

½ cup grated **Pecorino** cheese

Salt and freshly ground **black pepper**

KALE AND MUSTARD GREENS

SERVES 8 TO 10

In a large salad bowl, toss together the greens and pepitas. Drizzle the vinaigrette slowly on the greens, being careful not to overdress the salad, and toss. Top with cheese, toss again, and allow to sit for 10 minutes before serving. Season with salt and pepper to taste and toss again.

VEGETABLES

When your soups (or rice, or beans) need a salty crunch,
go for Kale Chips on Sunchoke Soup, Quick Pickles in
Bean Salad, or Kimchi atop Filipino Healing Soup. If the
kids refuse to eat carrot soup, they might happily eat
those same carrots roasted with butter and maple syrup.
When your vegetable bin is full and you've already made
your soup, just go on a roasting spree, and be generous
with the salt and pepper. Plants are tasty.

In the early fall when green beans are plentiful I eat them almost every day. Usually steamed and salted are just fine, but when I came across a variation by Pam Anderson (the chef, not the *Baywatch* babe), it transformed my simple green beans into quite a snazzy side dish and opened up the wonderful world of mustard cream sauce to many a protein and vegetable. I've adapted her recipe—no pearl onions, thank you, and I prefer half-and-half to butter—but the spirit is the same. // COURTNEY

1 cup slivered **almonds**

2 tablespoons **olive oil**

3 pounds **green beans**, trimmed

1 teaspoon **salt**, plus more to taste

4 **shallots**, thinly sliced

2 **garlic cloves**, minced

2 tablespoons dry **white wine**

¾ cup **chicken broth**

⅓ cup **Dijon mustard**

1 cup **half-and-half**

Freshly ground **black pepper**

GREEN BEANS WITH MUSTARD AND ALMONDS

SERVES 8 TO 10

Place the almonds in a dry large skillet and heat until fragrant, shaking or stirring to avoid burning. Remove from the pan as soon as their edges begin to brown.

// Add 1 tablespoon of the oil to the skillet. Add the green beans, ½ cup water, and the salt. Cover, bring to a boil, reduce the heat to a simmer, and cook over medium heat until the beans are bright green and still have a slight crunch, 7 to 10 minutes. Remove the beans and set aside.

// Wipe out the pan with a paper towel so it is dry. Heat the remaining tablespoon of oil in the skillet and add the shallots and garlic. Sauté until soft, 5 minutes. Add the wine, broth, and mustard to the pan. Stir with a flat whisk to combine and simmer, uncovered, for 5 minutes, or until the sauce has reduced by half and thickened. Add the half-and-half. Stir to combine.

// Add the beans to the pan and toss to coat them with the sauce. Sprinkle in the almonds and toss to combine. Season with salt and pepper to taste.

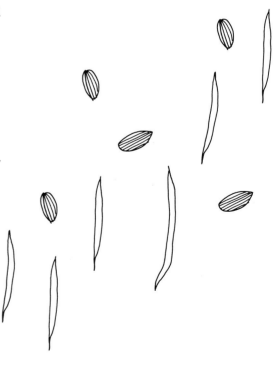

Kimchi, the fermented and pungent food, the national dish of Korea, is an all-purpose condiment for fifty percent of my household. I add it to chicken soups, pho, ramen, plain rice, fancy rice, sesame noodles, and my son eats it on hot dogs, his iteration of the sauerkraut our ancestors made and sold out of barrels, in our very neighborhood, about a century ago.

I got this great starter recipe from my friend David, who had the good sense to marry my friend Brooke. They split their time between Chicago and Kenmare, in the southwest of Ireland. Kenmare is a locavore-farm-to-table foodie heaven, but it's not so strong on the Asian markets, so David has gone completely *fermento* and is perhaps the only kimchi source in all of County Kerry. // CAROLINE

KIMCHI

MAKES 2 TO 3 PINTS

Mix the cabbage and scallions in a big bowl (and daikon, if using), and slowly add and mix in 1 tablespoon salt. Cover the ingredients with a dinner plate that is weighed down (by a can of beans or tomatoes, for example), and let sit for 3 to 6 hours. The cabbage will "sweat" out the water, aided by the salt and weight.

// Combine the seasonings in a small bowl and set aside.

// Using kitchen gloves, "knead" the vegetables for 5 to 7 minutes, trying to squeeze out as much water as possible into the bowl (do not discard the liquid). Add the seasonings to the vegetables and mix thoroughly.

// Fill the jars with vegetables, leaving 1 inch at the top of each jar. Spoon the remaining liquid into each jar, but do not fill above 1 inch from the top. Tightly cap the jars.

// Place the jars on a dish or pie plate (to catch any spills) and leave in a warm spot. Each morning loosen the lids for a few seconds to allow gases to escape, then tighten. Once a day, invert the jars for an hour. Then slightly loosen the lids and retighten.

// Wait 5 to 25 days, then refrigerate. Yes, that's a big range of days. Kimchi is ready to eat as soon as you like the flavor of it, much like pickles. A "new" kimchi won't be as pungent as a long-fermented one, so taste a little piece before refrigerating (which stops the fermentation) to determine how funky your palate is. Kimchi keeps several months in the refrigerator.

EQUIPMENT

3 wide-mouth pint-size **glass jars** with tight-fitting lids

1 very large **mixing bowl**

1 pair disposable **kitchen gloves**

KIMCHI VEGETABLES

2 medium to large heads **napa cabbage**, cored, outer leaves discarded, sliced in half lengthwise, each half sliced in thirds lengthwise and cut into 2-inch pieces

2 bunches **scallions**, outer layer removed, top 2 inches removed, sliced in half lengthwise and cut into 2-inch pieces

1 pound **daikon** or other radish, thinly sliced (optional)

Kosher **salt**

SEASONINGS

4 ounces minced **garlic**

4 ounces minced peeled fresh **ginger**

2 tablespoons **Asian fish sauce** (nam pla)

2 tablespoons **Korean chili pepper** flakes (Gochugaru)

3 pounds baby **carrots**, rinsed, or 3 pounds (about 24) carrots, sliced into ¾-inch disks

2 tablespoons **olive oil**

1 tablespoon **butter**

3 tablespoons pure **maple syrup**

½ teaspoon large-flake **sea salt**

In my house we eat these sweet buttery carrots straight from the skillet, unable to wait for them to get to the table. Finishing them with large-flake salt like Maldon balances the sweetness and makes them completely addictive. I like to make them in my cast-iron skillet to transfer seamlessly from oven to stovetop. Cast iron helps the outside of the carrots caramelize, adding a smoky flavor to each bite. // COURTNEY

MAPLE BUTTER CARROTS

SERVES 8 TO 10

Preheat the oven to 375°F.

// Toss the carrots in the olive oil in a large ovenproof sauté pan. Bake, stirring every 10 minutes, until all the carrots are tender and caramelized (about 40 minutes). Bring the pan to the stovetop and set over low heat. Add the butter and maple syrup and stir until they begin to foam. Continue to stir constantly, taking care to lower the heat if needed, until the maple butter sauce has thickened slightly and a spatula dragged across the bottom of the pan leaves a distinct trail. Remove the pan from the heat and sprinkle with the salt.

When tomatoes are in season it's hard to keep up with the bounty. So consider drying them when prices fall or when your CSA starts sending you home with pounds and pounds. Italians dried tomatoes by placing them on racks on their roofs and allowing the sun to desiccate them. Oven-drying tomatoes is simpler and requires no dangerous climbing, but do plan ahead because the oven will be occupied for hours. (Note that five pounds of fresh tomatoes yields about six ounces, or two cups, of dried tomatoes, which provides a real lesson in shrinkage.)

Use Oven-Dried Tomatoes to replace store-bought sun-dried tomatoes when making Greek Orzo (page 194) and Jeweled Rice Salad (page 192). // TINA

5 pounds large **tomatoes** (such as Roma or Beefsteak)

2 tablespoons **olive oil**

4 tablespoons minced **fresh herbs**, such as oregano, basil, or thyme

2 teaspoons **salt**

½ to 1 teaspoon freshly ground **black pepper**

OVEN-DRIED TOMATOES

MAKES ABOUT 2 CUPS

Preheat the oven to 200°F.

// Cut the tomatoes in half lengthwise and remove the core, seeds, and juices. Gently toss the tomatoes in a bowl with the olive oil, herbs, salt, and pepper. Lay out the tomatoes on rimmed baking sheets, cut side up. The skins will dry out best if they are not touching.

// Bake until the tomatoes shrivel and feel dry. This can take anywhere from 8 to 10 hours. Check the tomatoes from time to time: They should remain flexible and not become brittle. If the sides of any tomatoes are starting to brown, remove them from the sheet.

// Remove from the oven and cool completely before storing in a zipper bag or container. Keep them in the refrigerator for up to 1 week, or freeze to use when needed.

BREADS, GRAINS & PASTAS

This is a really big category. Some recipes are so integral to soup, like Cheddar Cornbread with any of the chilis, that they are included in soup delivery instructions. Many of the grains are ideal for lining a bowl of soup like Spinach Polenta (page 199) with Sun-Dried Tomato Soup (page 98) or Coconut Rice and Beans (page 189) with Thai Fish Curry (page 124). Sesame Noodles (page 198) and Jeweled Rice (page 192) can be stand-alone meals or very substantial sides.

Let's be honest: Everyone loves a good carb.

A leftover baguette is a crostini waiting to happen! And just about every soup is an invitation for a piece or two of crostini. For a variation, try with Chive-Studded Chèvre (recipe follows). // JULIE

2 **baguettes**, sliced into 15 to 16 pieces per loaf

6 to 8 tablespoons **olive oil**

4 **garlic cloves**, minced (optional)

Coarse salt

Freshly ground **black pepper**

CROSTINI

MAKES 30 TO 32 PIECES

Preheat the oven to 400°F.

// Lay the sliced bread on two rimmed baking sheets and lightly brush with the olive oil and the minced garlic, if using. Season with coarse salt and freshly ground pepper. Bake for 5 to 7 minutes, or until just lightly golden. Remove and let cool.

Chive-Studded Chèvre

MAKES 1 POUND

This herb-infused cheese spread on crostini can add incredible flavor and creaminess to soups and salads. I always serve it with Roasted Parsnip Soup (page 85), but it pairs well with many others. Look for good-quality fresh chèvre (a soft goat cheese). It will definitely make a difference. // JULIE

1 pound **chèvre**, at room temperature

1 bunch **chives**, finely diced

Place the chèvre and chives in a medium bowl and stir well to combine. When well integrated, roll the chèvre into a log and wrap in plastic wrap. Refrigerate until ready to use. Once the cheese log is fully chilled, you can slice off sections to deliver with a soup or to serve on a cheese plate.

SQUASH
BREAD

This is best made in a twelve-inch cast-iron skillet so the bread gets that great crust that comes from cooking in cast iron. You can never go wrong with a side of cornbread. // COURTNEY

CHEDDAR CORNBREAD

MAKES ONE 12-INCH SKILLET; SERVES 8 TO 10

2 cups **all-purpose flour**, sifted

2 cups **yellow cornmeal**

3 tablespoons **baking powder**

1 teaspoon **salt**

2 **eggs**

2 cups **milk**

8 tablespoons unsalted **butter**, at room temperature

8 ounces **cream cheese**, at room temperature

1 cup shredded **cheddar cheese**

Preheat the oven to 400°F. Place an ungreased 12-inch cast-iron pan in the oven for 15 minutes.

// In a large bowl, combine the flour, cornmeal, baking powder, and salt. In a small bowl, beat the eggs and milk together. Set aside.

// In a small saucepan, melt 7 tablespoons of the butter and add the cream cheese and cheddar. Stir slowly over low heat until creamy and combined.

// Add the cheese and butter mixture to the dry ingredients, then pour in the milk-and-egg mixture. Stir to combine but don't overstir. The batter should be thick but pourable.

// Using potholders and being careful not to burn yourself, carefully remove the pan from the oven and drop the remaining tablespoon of butter into the hot pan. Tilt the pan around until the butter melts and coats the bottom. Immediately pour in the batter, scraping down the sides of the bowl with a flexible spatula.

// Bake for 20 to 25 minutes, or until a knife inserted into the middle of the bread comes out clean. Let the cornbread cool in the pan, or serve while still warm.

2 cups **Roasted Squash**, mashed (recipe follows), made with butternut squash or pumpkin, or canned 100% pumpkin puree

4 **eggs**, beaten

¾ cup **neutral oil**

½ cup unsweetened **applesauce**

1 tablespoon freshly squeezed **lemon juice**

1 cup **brown sugar**, packed

¾ cup **granulated sugar**

2 cups **all-purpose flour**

1 cup plus 2 tablespoons **whole-wheat flour**

2 teaspoons **baking soda**

1½ teaspoons **salt**

1 teaspoon ground **cinnamon**

½ teaspoon ground **ginger**

2 to 3 teaspoons ground **cardamom**

1 to 2 cups chopped pecans or **walnuts**

2 tablespoons turbinado **sugar**

1 large tart **apple**, such as Granny Smith, cored and cut into ⅛-inch-thick slices, or ½ **delicata squash**, scrubbed and thinly sliced, crosswise with the skin on

Winter squash, cut in half and seeds removed

When winter squash begin to proliferate in the late summer to mid-winter, I feel under no pressure to cook it up right away. It's called winter squash not because it is harvested in the winter, but because it lasts well into winter. Acorn, butternut, buttercup, carnival, delicata, kabocha, sweet dumpling . . . the names of these winter varieties alone inspire, and I love having squash on hand to make soups and loaves of squash bread. // TINA

SQUASH BREAD

MAKES FOUR MINI OR TWO STANDARD LOAVES

Preheat the oven to 350°F. Grease and flour 4 mini or two 8½ by 5½-inch loaf pans.

// In a large bowl, mix together the mashed squash, eggs, oil, applesauce, ¼ cup water, the lemon juice, and the brown and granulated sugars until blended.

// In a separate bowl, mix together the flours, baking soda, salt, cinnamon, ginger, and 1 teaspoon of the ground cardamom. Stir the dry ingredients into the squash mixture until just blended. Gently fold in the nuts. Divide among the pans.

// In a small bowl, mix the turbinado sugar with 1 to 2 teaspoons of ground cardamom, to taste.

// Sprinkle the loaves with cardamom sugar, about 1 tablespoon per loaf (or ½ tablespoon each for the mini loaves). Decorate the tops of each loaf with some slices of apple or delicata squash.

// Bake mini loaves for about 45 minutes and larger loaves for 65 to 75 minutes, or until a toothpick comes out clean.

Roasted Squash

It's really hard to know how much your squash will yield: cavity sizes, water weight, and number of seeds vary considerably. A small squash can yield as little as 1 cup. One giant 6¼-pound butternut squash once yielded nearly 9 cups of squash puree. It's nice to have a few squash recipes so that you can make use of it all if you end up with too much. You can roast the squash ahead of time and refrigerate the flesh for three to four days, or freeze it for up to six months. Try pumpkin and other varieties of squash and see which you prefer.

Preheat the oven to 400°F.

// Place the squash halves cut side down on a lightly greased rimmed baking sheet. Roast for 30 to 60 minutes, or until a fork slides easily into the flesh of the thickest part of the squash. (For butternut squash, this is the side without the seeds and cavity; for pumpkin, kabocha, delicata, and others, look for the thickest wall.) Cool, peel, and scoop out the roasted flesh.

3 **eggs**

1 cup **sugar**

1 cup **canola oil**

1 tablespoon **pure vanilla extract**

2 cups grated **zucchini**, from about
  2 medium unpeeled zucchinis

2 cups **all-purpose flour**

1 cup **whole-wheat flour**

1 teaspoon **baking soda**

¼ teaspoon **baking powder**

1 teaspoon **salt**

1½ teaspoons ground **cinnamon**

1 cup chopped **walnuts**, lightly toasted

¾ cup unsweetened **shredded coconut**

¾ cup semisweet or bittersweet
  chocolate chips

———————

If the idea of turning on your oven in the summer heat during Crazy Squash Time is unappealing, freeze 2-cup portions of grated zucchini in freezer zipper bags and save for more appropriate baking weather.

During high summer, aka Crazy Squash Time, I bake zucchini bread, following in the footsteps of my grandma Irene. My version adheres more closely to my mom's recipe, but I've added dark chocolate chips and coconut. I don't think there's a more perfect companion to afternoon coffee or to have for dessert with a dollop of whipped cream, and the kids love it as a snack. // JULIE

ZUCCHINI BREAD

MAKES TWO LOAVES

Preheat the oven to 325°F. Grease and flour two 8½ by 5½-inch loaf pans.

// In a large bowl, beat the eggs until light and foamy using an electric hand mixer or a stand mixer. Then beat in the sugar and oil until well combined. Mix in the vanilla and zucchini.

// In a medium bowl, mix together the flours, baking soda, baking powder, salt, and cinnamon. Add to the wet ingredients and stir to combine.

// Gently stir in the nuts, coconut, and chocolate chips until just incorporated and divide between the two loaf pans.

// Bake for 50 to 60 minutes, or until a toothpick inserted in the center comes out clean. Cool for 10 minutes in the pans and then turn the loaves out onto a baking rack to cool completely.

Early on in our adolescence my sister, Stephanie, and I went vegetarian, motivated (on my part) by slightly more rebelliousness than mindfulness. My mother found a meat-free cookbook put out by a local animal shelter, and it contained this corn casserole recipe, with an unforgettable shopping list: A Can, A Can, A Stick, A Box, and An Egg. It won't win any nutrition awards, but Corn Casserole has many other virtues. It's delicious, it's almost impossible to mess up, it's easily enhanced, and you can find the ingredients anywhere. Its place on all our family's tables has long outlasted our vegetarianism.

It's a forgiving recipe, so when you make it as a side dish (at Thanksgiving, for example) and you have other food that needs a higher or lower cooking temperature, that's fine. Just stick this in the oven, and check it at thirty minutes and at five-minute intervals after that until a knife comes out clean, keeping in mind that the depth of the vessel you're cooking in will affect the timing. For Soup Club, I prepare corn casserole in mini loaf pans. At home, I like to serve it out of my deeper, pumpkin-shaped enameled cast-iron pot. It works in a nine-inch square baking dish. Or a pie plate, or a regular cast-iron pan. I have substituted frozen corn kernels for the canned stuff, but the creamed corn has to be from a can, or the magic is lost. // CAROLINE

CORN CASSEROLE

SERVES 8 TO 10

Preheat the oven to 375°F. Grease the bottom and sides of the baking pan, using a little bit of the softened butter.

// Combine all the ingredients directly in the baking pan, and whisk to combine. Bake for 45 minutes, or until a knife inserted in the center comes out clean.

1 15.25-ounce can **sweet corn**, drained (or 2 cups **frozen corn** kernels, thawed)

1 15.25-ounce can **creamed corn**

1 stick (½ cup) **butter**, very soft

1 8.5-ounce **box corn muffin mix**

1 **egg**, lightly beaten

Variations to Add into the Batter Before Cooking

Mild and Cheesy Add 1 finely chopped red bell pepper and 1 cup shredded cheese (sharp cheddar works especially well). Sprinkle a little more shredded cheese on the top about halfway through cooking.

Spicy Add ½ teaspoon cayenne pepper or ½ cup pickled jalapeños or Hatch green chilies.

Meaty Dice 4 ounces spicy dry chorizo and sauté for 5 minutes, until it starts to shrivel and give off its oil, then add to the batter. Or 1 cup cooked, chopped, or crumbled sweet Italian sausage, fresh chorizo, regular hot dogs (especially popular with kids), or veggie dogs.

Beans 1 cup cooked (or canned) drained beans. Edamame and little black beans look good dotted throughout.

FOR THE DILL-ALMOND-LEMON PESTO

3 cups tightly packed **dill leaves** (stems discarded)

1 cup sliced **almonds**, toasted

2 **garlic cloves**, minced

½ cup grated **Parmigiano-Reggiano**

¾ cup **olive oil**

2 tablespoons freshly squeezed **lemon juice**, plus more to taste

1 teaspoon **salt**, plus more to taste

FOR THE COUSCOUS

3 cups **Israeli** or **pearl couscous** (about 1 pound)

1½ cups sliced **almonds**, toasted (page 50)

3 cups seeded, sliced, and quartered **cucumbers** (about 3 cucumbers)

———————

Israeli couscous (sometimes called pearl couscous) is much larger than the familiar small North African couscous. Serve this as a bed for baked salmon.

This dish is a tribute to both sides of my family. My dad was born on the Lower East Side of Manhattan and moved to Israel when he was still a boy. He and my mom met on a ship crossing the Atlantic from Scandinavia to New York. My mom is Danish, and in Denmark dill is held in high regard, so I've used it instead of parsley, which is most often associated with couscous salads. It's a harmonious blend, punctuated by almonds and cucumber, a true Danish-Israeli union. // TINA

DILLED ISRAELI COUSCOUS

SERVES 8 TO 10

Bring 2 quarts well-salted water to a boil.

// Meanwhile, make the pesto by blending together all the pesto ingredients in a food processor until smooth.

// Add couscous to the boiling water. Reduce the heat and simmer, uncovered, for about 8 minutes, or until the couscous is al dente. Immediately drain and rinse with cold water after cooking.

// Add the pesto to the cooled couscous, and toss to coat. Mix in the toasted almonds and the quartered cucumbers.

// The salad keeps well for 1 to 2 days in the refrigerator. When ready to serve, adjust the salt and spritz with additional lemon juice.

This classic West Indian side is a mellow counterpoint to the heavily spiced Curried Goat (page 202) and Thai Fish Curry (page 124). It's almost like a savory rice pudding and the leftovers make great rice pancakes, mixed with a beaten egg and fried. // CAROLINE

COCONUT RICE AND BEANS

SERVES 8 TO 10

2 tablespoons **butter**, **coconut oil**, or **ghee** (see page 22)

2 medium **yellow onions**, finely chopped

2 tablespoons fresh **thyme** leaves

5 cups long-grain **brown rice**

3 13.5-ounce cans **coconut milk**, well stirred

2 15.5-ounce cans **pigeon peas** (or red kidney beans), drained and rinsed

2 teaspoons **salt**

2 teaspoons freshly ground **black pepper**

Heat the butter or oil in a large, wide pot, such as a Dutch oven or braiser. Sauté the onions until soft, and add the thyme and rice. Stir the rice to combine with the onions, and then add the coconut milk. Fill the three empty cans with cold water and add those too (that's 40.5 ounces of water, if you've already sent the cans to recycling), then turn the heat up to high until the pot comes to a boil.

// Add the pigeon peas to the pot, along with the salt and pepper. Stir to combine, reduce the heat to low, cover the pot, and let simmer for 45 minutes. Check that the liquid has been absorbed and the rice is fully cooked. Turn off the heat and let the rice and beans sit, covered, until ready to serve.

One brisk spring day, Julie and I were taking our kids up to Tompkins Square, a park and playground worth the trek out of our neighborhood. As we pushed our heavy double strollers along the uneven, empty sidewalks, I noticed a twenty-dollar bill lying in the middle of the street. The meaning was clear: Some benevolent force was treating us to free cappuccinos from Abraço, a tiny, terrific coffee bar on Seventh Street, and enough of their sweet-salty shortbread to go around.

Alas, twenty-dollar bills do *not* sprout like weeds out of the New York City concrete, so I made up my own shortbread at home. Black olive shortbread has a bit of goofy intrigue: To the uninitiated, it looks sort of like a chocolate chip cookie . . . until the first salty bite. It elevates both strong coffee and red wine. I serve it with Chestnut Soup (page 78), and I like to give people the dough, frozen in logs, for future easy baking. // CAROLINE

1 pound (4 sticks) unsalted **butter**, softened

1½ cups **sugar**

2 **egg yolks** (reserve the whites to make Sweet and Spicy Nuts, page 234)

3½ cups **all-purpose flour**

½ cup **cornstarch**

2 cups (8 ounces) pitted and finely chopped **black oil-cured olives**

BLACK OLIVE SHORTBREAD

MAKES 3 TO 4 DOZEN

Using an electric hand mixer or a stand mixer, cream the butter and sugar, then add the egg yolks. Once combined, add the flour and cornstarch. Stir in the olives using a wooden spoon.

// Split the dough into 2 even pieces and roll them each into a log 1½ to 2 inches in diameter. Wrap in plastic wrap and chill for at least 30 minutes. (You can use an empty paper towel tube that is cut open lengthwise to hold the chilled dough. This will prevent the logs from flattening on one side.) You can also freeze the dough, tightly wrapped in cellophane or wax paper, and stored in a zipper bag, for up to 6 months.

// When you're ready to bake, preheat the oven to 275°F.

// Slice the chilled dough (straight from the freezer is fine) into thick circles (about ¼ inch); they're so crumbly that the thinner ones just fall apart. Set them on a parchment-lined cookie sheet. They can be close together because they don't spread out much. Bake for 25 to 30 minutes, until they're just starting to look a little golden brown. Let cool on the cookie sheet for a few minutes, then transfer to a wire rack.

3 cups uncooked **short-grain brown rice**

Lemon Dressing (page 153)

6 to 8 **scallions**, finely chopped

1 cup finely chopped fresh **flat-leaf parsley**

1 cup chopped **pecans**, toasted

1½ cups **red grapes**, sliced in half

1½ cups **grape tomatoes**, sliced in half

Salt and freshly ground **black pepper**

———

ALSO TRY

Dried cherries, mint, and pistachios

Dried cranberries, mustard greens, and almonds

Figs, pine nuts, basil, and oven-dried tomatoes (page 177)

I originally discovered a delicious rice salad in *The Moosewood Cookbook*, my first vegetarian tome. Nearly fifteen years and many variations later, I still love the balance of tart lemon dressing, sweet grapes, and pecans. You can make this with toasted walnuts and dried apricots instead, and throw in extra vegetables.

Enjoy with any of the chilled soups (see page 112) and the Honey, Ricotta, and Black Pepper Bruschetta (page 232). // JULIE

JEWELED RICE

SERVES 8 TO 10

Put the rice and 4½ cups cold water in a saucepan. Bring to a boil, then cover and reduce the heat to the lowest possible simmer and cook without disturbing for 35 minutes, or until all the water is absorbed and the rice is tender. Transfer the rice to a rimmed baking sheet and spread it out evenly. This will allow the rice to cool evenly and keep the grains separate. Cool completely.

// Transfer the rice to a large bowl and coat with the lemon dressing. Stir in the scallions, parsley, pecans, grapes, and tomatoes. Season with salt and pepper .

// Serve immediately, or cover tightly and refrigerate. The salad is even better the second day.

16 ounces **orzo**

Salt

2 tablespoons **olive oil**

½ **red onion**, quartered and thinly sliced

1 cup **Oven-Dried Tomatoes** (page 177) or **sun-dried tomatoes**, sliced into strips

1 cup **pine nuts**, toasted (see page 50)

1 bunch **flat-leaf parsley**, finely chopped (about 1 cup)

½ cup minced fresh **mint**

2 tablespoons minced fresh **oregano leaves**

2 cups **feta cheese**, crumbled or diced into ¼-inch cubes

Lemon-Shallot Vinaigrette (page 152)

Freshly ground **black pepper**

2 cups fresh **baby spinach**, packed

Orzo, which means "barley" in Italian, is shaped like a giant grain of rice, but it's actually pasta. This version is Greek, but you can take this versatile pasta in many flavor directions. In general, cook the orzo (and all pastas used in salads) al dente so that it can drink up some of the dressing without becoming mushy. // TINA

GREEK ORZO

SERVES 8 TO 10

Add the orzo to a pot of well-salted boiling water and cook for 7 to 9 minutes, until al dente. Rinse with cold water to remove excess starch and toss with the olive oil to prevent sticking.

// In a large bowl, assemble the salad by adding the red onion, tomatoes, pine nuts, herbs, and feta cheese. Mix in the vinaigrette, starting with ½ cup. Toss to coat. Season with salt and pepper to taste. Add the fresh baby spinach right before serving or delivery.

Years ago, my Aunt Lisa, mother to six young children, excitedly announced that she had purchased a wheat berry grinder so that she could bake her own bread from the wheat berries that she would grind each day. She continued this bread-baking journey for years, grinding wheat and baking fresh bread daily for her big and hungry family. As a mother of three now, I can't even imagine doing that, but I do love wheat berries, and cooking with them always reminds me of my aunt's commitment to nutrition and cooking from scratch.

Enjoy this tender, nutty grain stirred into Senegalese Peanut Soup (page 101), Thai Fish Curry (page 124), or Carrot Coconut Soup (page 75). It also accompanies grilled fish and meats well. // JULIE

COCONUT WHEAT BERRIES WITH HERBS

SERVES 8 TO 10

1½ pounds (or 4 cups) uncooked **wheat berries** (look for a variety that has not been pearled)

3 13.5-ounce cans unsweetened **coconut milk**, well stirred

½ cup unsweetened shredded **coconut**

2 teaspoons **salt**, plus more to taste

1 cup finely chopped **fresh herbs** (flat-leaf parsley, mint, chives, thyme, or a mixture)

Freshly ground **black pepper**

Pick over the wheat berries, discarding stones or debris, and rinse well in a colander under cold water. Add the wheat berries, 7 cups cold water, coconut milk, coconut, and salt to a medium pot, and bring to a boil. Reduce the heat and simmer, covered. Start checking for doneness after about 30 minutes. The texture should be tender but still slightly chewy. The wheat berries may take up to 25 more minutes, so plan to check their texture every 5 minutes or so.

// When the wheat berries are al dente, drain and pour off any excess liquid and transfer the wheat berries to a medium bowl. Stir in the chopped herbs until well mixed. Season with salt and pepper.

// Serve warm or at room temperature.

SEWARD PARK GARDEN

One August evening, I started to make a chowder with some perfect, huge ears of corn. My husband stole a taste from the pot, just before I added in the broth, and told me to stop. Sometimes your soup wants to be something else, and this dish was done. We ate it over mustard greens, topped with a runny fried egg; garlic-rubbed sourdough bread and some perfect tomatoes made it a memorable meal. Husking the corn and shaving off all those kernels is a labor of love, but this is a worthy main course for dinner or even brunch. It would be a great way to thank those friends who invited you for the weekend. After some debate over whether to call it risotto-style corn or corn caviar or corn stew, Ian decided it was truly a humble hash. You can only make this when corn is in peak season—sweet, cheap, and abundant—so be ready to seize the moment. // **CAROLINE**

SUMMER CORN HASH

SERVES 8

In a large pan or Dutch oven with a lid, sauté the bacon over medium heat for 10 to 15 minutes, until the fat starts to render and the bacon pieces start to look cooked.

// Add the onions, leeks, and hot peppers and sauté for 5 to 10 more minutes, stirring occasionally, until softened. Add the corn kernels and salt, and continue cooking for 5 more minutes.

// Add the broth, cover the pan, turn the heat to low, and cook for 5 minutes. Remove from heat and add black pepper to taste and more salt, if needed. Stir in the crème fraîche, basil, and parsley. Cover and let sit until ready to serve.

// To serve, toss the bitter greens with just a little walnut vinaigrette. Fry the eggs so the whites are set but the yolks are runny. Line each bowl with the greens. Cover the greens with corn hash and top with an egg. Season with salt and pepper to taste. Toast slices of the sourdough bread and rub the warm toast with the cut surface of the garlic or tomato, if using. Serve with the hash.

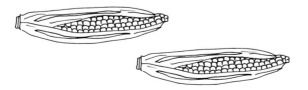

1½ pounds best-quality thick-sliced **bacon**, diced

2 large red **onions**, finely chopped

8 large **leeks**, trimmed and washed, white and light green parts finely chopped

4 medium-hot **peppers**, such as jalapeños, finely chopped

20 ears **corn**, kernels only, approximately 16 cups (freeze the cobs for Winter Corn Chowder, page 93)

2 teaspoons **salt**

1 cup hot **chicken broth** or **vegetable broth** (homemade preferred, page 30, if you have it on hand)

Freshly ground **black pepper**

½ cup **Crème Fraîche** (page 47)

½ cup tightly packed fresh **basil leaves**, finely sliced

½ cup tightly packed fresh **flat-leaf parsley leaves**, chopped

2 large bunches **bitter greens**, such as mustard greens, frisée, arugula, or dandelion, thinly sliced (about 10 cups)

Walnut Vinaigrette (page 152)

8 **eggs**, or 1 per person

Sourdough bread

1 **garlic** clove, peeled and halved (optional)

1 small **tomato**, halved (optional)

THE WEEKENDER

If you invite us to stay for the weekend, Ian will make you his signature cocktail to enjoy, pre-hash. For each cocktail, mix two parts bourbon or Tennessee whiskey (George Dickel, if you can find it) with one part blood orange soda (like San Pellegrino Aranciata Rosso). Add several dashes of bitters and a squeeze of fresh lime juice. Top with a splash of seltzer. Serve on the rocks.

1 tablespoon **salt**

8 **garlic cloves**, finely chopped

8 sprigs **thyme**, leaves only

2 tablespoons ground **allspice**

2 tablespoons ground **cumin**

1 small **Thai chili pepper**, finely chopped

5 tablespoons yellow **curry powder**, divided

4 **limes**, quartered, plus more lime wedges for serving

6 to 7 pounds bone-in **goat stew meat**, cubed (or lamb or beef)

3 tablespoons **vegetable oil**

1 large **yellow onion**, finely chopped

6 **jalapeño peppers**, sliced, pith and seeds removed for a milder flavor if desired

2 **green bell peppers**, cored, seeded, and diced

18 **scallions**, roughly chopped

1 13.5-ounce can unsweetened **coconut milk**, well stirred

Coconut Rice and Beans (page 189)

1 bunch fresh **cilantro**, leaves only

There was a particularly cold November morning when I needed to make a stew. Our buildings were in the blackout zone, post–Hurricane Sandy, but thankfully our wonder-friend Jason (of Brussels sprouts fame) took in our family for the week. I was happy to return home when the lights and electricity came back on, but we still had no heat or hot water, so I roasted and baked and simmered to keep out the chill. Thankfully, the gas stove was working. Thanks also go to Silva, the butcher at Heritage Meats in Essex Market, who encouraged me to give goat a try. It was in season, and, Silva assured me, a perfect stew meat for his house-and-bone-warming recipe for West Indian curry—a dish of Thanksgiving. Start this recipe two days in advance, if possible, to give the goat a day to marinate and the stew a day to sit and deepen. // CAROLINE

CURRIED GOAT

SERVES 8 TO 10

Create a rub by combining the salt, garlic, thyme, allspice, cumin, and Thai chili in a bowl. Add 2 tablespoons of the curry powder and squeeze in the juice from 3 limes.

// Soak the goat in a large bowl of cold water to rinse off any particles of bone dust left over from the butchering. Drain the goat and pat dry with paper towels. Rub the remaining lime wedges over the goat pieces. In a large bowl or zipper bag, coat the goat with the spice rub, throw in the lime rinds, and let sit in the refrigerator, covered, for at least 6 hours or up to 2 days.

// When you're ready to cook, let the goat come to room temperature and preheat the oven to 350°F.

// In a large Dutch oven, heat the oil and add the onion, jalapeños, bell peppers, scallions, and the remaining 3 tablespoons of curry powder. Cook until the curry gets very aromatic and the onions and peppers start to soften, about 7 minutes, stirring occasionally and making sure not to let the curry powder burn.

// Increase the heat to medium high. Push the vegetables to one side and, working in batches, add the goat to the pot (reserving the spice rub liquid), browning the meat on each side. Return all the goat to the pot, add one cup of cold water, cover, and continue to cook for about 15 minutes, until the meat starts to break up.

// Discard the lime rinds, and add the remaining spice rub liquid, the coconut milk, and enough water so that the meat is just sitting in liquid (it doesn't need to be covered). Bring to a boil on the stove, then cover loosely with foil and transfer to the oven. Cook for an hour, or until the meat is fork-tender and easily pulls away from the bone.

// To serve, make a mound of rice and beans in each bowl, and scoop the goat into the middle, making sure to get plenty of curry broth from the pot. Top with cilantro and pass around lime wedges to spritz on top.

GOAT NOTE

Besides providing delicious meat—a little earthy and rich-tasting, though lower in fat and cholesterol than chicken, beef, or pork—goats are easy on the earth. They eat grasses and flowers without trampling those crops to death, and because of their picky palate, they are not practical feedlot animals. Caribbean markets will often carry goat, but it's always worth asking your local butcher, too.

2½ tablespoons **fennel seeds**

1½ tablespoons **salt**

1 teaspoon dried **oregano**

1 teaspoon dried **basil**

1 teaspoon dried **rosemary**

¾ teaspoon **red pepper flakes**

7½ pounds bone-in **pork shoulder**, no skin but fat layer intact

3 tablespoons **olive oil**

8 to 10 **garlic cloves**, minced

4 cups **chicken broth** or white wine

2 tablespoons unsalted **butter**

On lazy weekend afternoons there is nothing that quite hits the spot like a porchetta sandwich. Richly seasoned with bits of crunchy skin to contrast with juicy meat, it needs no condiment and is best accompanied by a cold hoppy beer or tart lemonade. Porchetta, an Italian dish, is traditionally made by roasting skin-on pork belly wrapped around a seasoned pork loin. When I can't make it to the aptly named Porchetta store in my neighborhood, I have found this recipe, a riff on Jeanne Kelley's 2010 recipe in *Bon Appétit*, to be a good stand-in. This recipe uses one piece of pork shoulder with a garlic rub and a crust of spices to replace the crackling skin on the original. Boneless shoulder is easier to slice, but I've also used bone-in to great result. Loosely tenting the meat with foil while in the oven and adding some liquid to baste the meat keeps the roast from drying out, a cross between a braise and a roast.

Start a day ahead or at the least in the morning, and roast in the late afternoon so the spices and garlic have had a chance to sit on the meat for a while. Serve with Braised Leafy Greens with Egg (page 172). // COURTNEY

PORCHETTA-ESQUE PORK BUTT WITH QUICK PAN SAUCE

SERVES 8 TO 10

Toast the fennel seeds in a dry pan until fragrant, approximately 3 minutes.

// Cool the fennel seeds. Once cool, place them in a spice grinder and add the salt, oregano, basil, rosemary, and red pepper flakes. Grind until sandy in texture. You can also use a mortar and pestle for grinding.

// Rinse the pork in cold water and dry it with paper towels. Rub the roast with 1 tablespoon of the olive oil and the minced garlic, coating all sides. Using a large spoon, sprinkle the spice mixture over all sides of the pork and press it to coat.

// Place the pork on a platter or large plate and cover loosely with plastic wrap or aluminum foil. Refrigerate overnight or up to 30 hours.

// Preheat the oven to 450°F.

// Remove the pork from the refrigerator and transfer to an oiled ovenproof roasting pan.

// Drizzle 1 to 2 tablespoons of the oil over the top of the pork and roast it fat side up for 30 minutes.

// Reduce the oven temperature to 325°F and add 1 cup of the chicken broth or wine (or a mix of the two) to the pan. Cover the pan loosely with foil and roast, checking periodically to ensure the liquid has not evaporated completely, adding more as needed. Baste every 1½ hours. Roast for 6½ to 7 hours, or until the pork reaches an internal temperature of 190°F and is falling off the bone.

// Once the porchetta is done, make a quick pan sauce: Transfer the porchetta to a platter and set aside. Pour the pan juices into a medium glass bowl. Spoon the fat from the top. Heat the roasting pan on the stove over medium heat. Add 2 tablespoons butter and 1 cup broth or wine. Scrape the bits from the bottom of the pan and stir constantly until it reduces slightly. Pour in the pan juices and simmer for 2 minutes. Remove the pan from the heat.

// To serve, reheat the pork and pass around the warmed-up pan sauce.

CAROLINE: I would be happy getting Courtney's Porchetta-esque Pork Butt on a weekly basis, for all the meal possibilities it provides (like Faux Ramen, page 40, or mixed into The Dudes' Chili, page 68). But I also really love the opportunity it gives me to say: I love Courtney's Butt. Hey Courtney, will you look at my Butt, and tell me if I'm doing this right? Let's try each other's Butts and compare notes. You know, that kind of thing.

Early one evening, my husband called me in a panic to tell me that a gas leak had been detected in our apartment building and the supply of cooking gas to the building was being shut off for "an undetermined length of time." I couldn't imagine how a tiny hot plate could service a family's worth of meals for weeks. Then I remembered my slow cooker. This chicken is my daughter's favorite dinner, so it is on regular rotation at our house. It requires no presautéing and needs to simmer for a while, so I decided to give it a go. It turns out it is a great slow cooker dish, so you can either follow the instructions below for stovetop cooking or set your slow cooker to high and increase the cooking time to 1 hour. I serve the sauce over rice, but you could also use it to dress cooked greens. Serve with Soy-Sesame Cucumber Salad (page 155). // COURTNEY

2 ounces fresh **ginger**, peeled and sliced into ¼-inch-thick coins

2 whole **scallions**

¼ cup **wine** (use any red or white wine you have around or vermouth)

⅔ cup **soy sauce**

4 pounds **chicken wings**, tips removed and saved for stock, or 5 pounds bone-in skin-on chicken thighs

1½ teaspoons **sugar**

8 to 12 cups cooked **white** or **brown rice**

SOY-SIMMERED CHICKEN WINGS

SERVES 8 TO 10

Place the ginger, scallions, wine, and soy sauce in a large Dutch oven or braising pan. Stir to combine. Add the chicken in a single layer. It is okay if the pieces touch. Turn the chicken to coat all pieces with the sauce. Use tongs to make it easy. Bring to a boil over high heat.

// Add ¼ cup water and return to a boil. Cover and cook over medium-low heat for 35 minutes, turning several times during cooking until the chicken is dark brown from the soy sauce and the meat is firm when poked with a fork.

// Remove from the heat and add the sugar. Stir to dissolve and coat the chicken with the sauce. Return to medium-low heat and cook, uncovered, for an additional 5 minutes.

// Remove the chicken from the sauce and set aside to cool, then refrigerate.

// Cool the sauce to room temperature. Remove and discard the scallions and ginger from the sauce. (Optional: Refrigerate the sauce 6 to 8 hours, until the fat solidifies and can be skimmed from the top. The sauce is gelatinous when cold but will liquefy when reheated.)

// To serve, reheat the sauce in a large saucepan. Add the chicken, cover, and bring to a simmer. Cook for 10 minutes, or until the chicken is heated through. The sauce will remain thin and can be spooned over rice.

2 pounds **sausage links** (such as merguez, spicy Italian, or boudin blanc)

Olive oil

4 **celery stalks**, chopped

3 large **carrots**, sliced diagonally into ½-inch-thick ovals

6 large **leeks**, trimmed and washed, white and light green parts finely chopped (3 large **onions** can substitute)

10 **garlic cloves**, minced

¼ cup **tomato paste**

1 pound **arugula** (or leafy green of your choice, such as broccoli rabe, chard, kale, or collards)

1 cup **red wine**

1 pound **lentils** (preferably black beluga or French green), rinsed and drained in a colander

2 sprigs **rosemary**, tied in a bundle with kitchen twine

6 large sprigs **thyme**, leaves only

Salt and freshly ground **black pepper**

Red pepper flakes

1 large bunch **flat-leaf parsley**, chopped

Fancy **olive oil**

Sherry vinegar

Dijon mustard (optional)

1 pound **salad greens**

Sourdough bread

1 **garlic clove**, halved (optional)

You can omit the sausages entirely **FOR A VEGETARIAN STEW**, but consider roasting a big pan of assorted mushrooms instead, tossed with olive oil, salt, and pepper, and add a piece of Parmesan rind while the lentils simmer.

I had a memorable version of this dish on a New Year's day in Italy, where it's traditionally eaten just after midnight for luck in the coming year. I don't think of myself as superstitious, but I've made it a point to have lentils on New Year's day ever since. Courtney, Julie, and Tina can attest that I've also fobbed off quarts on them, usually around December 31, as this is a stew that travels just as easily as soup (it's extremely dense, so one quart per household is plenty). Merguez, the highly seasoned lamb sausage, is a favorite of mine, but this dish adapts to other sausages as well as to other beans. Go Spanish with chickpeas, chorizo, and spinach, or Southern with black-eyed peas, andouille, and collards—another luck-filled trio. // CAROLINE

LENTIL-SAUSAGE STEW

SERVES 8

Preheat the oven to 400°F.

// Heat a large Dutch oven or deep-sided frying pan over medium heat. Prick the sausages and brown them on both sides. Transfer to the oven and roast for 25 minutes, until they are cooked through. Remove sausages to a plate.

// Add a tablespoon of olive oil to the Dutch oven, then add the celery, carrots, leeks, and garlic and sauté until soft. Stir in the tomato paste and cook until it starts to darken a bit.

// Meanwhile, if using broccoli rabe, collards, kale, or chard, blanch them first: Bring a pot of salted water to a boil, and briefly immerse the greens. Kale and chard need only about 30 seconds, collards about 2 minutes, and the broccoli rabe 5 minutes. Have a bowl of very cold water (with some ice cubes in it) ready nearby. When the greens are ready, remove from the pot and plunge it into the cold water to shock. Drain the greens, chop into bite-size pieces, and set aside.

// Add the wine to the tomato mixture and deglaze the pan, scraping up the brown bits with a wooden spoon. Stir in the lentils; add the rosemary sprigs, thyme leaves, a large pinch of salt, a few grinds of black pepper, and a pinch of red pepper flakes; and pour in 3 cups of cold water to cover the lentils by about an inch.

// Bring to a boil, reduce the heat, loosely cover, and simmer for about 30 minutes, adding more water if needed to keep the lentils just covered in liquid.

// When the lentils are done, remove the rosemary sprigs. Stir in the parsley and arugula (or other greens) and the cooked sausages, cut into bite-size pieces. Drizzle with fancy olive oil and add a tiny splash of sherry vinegar. Season with salt and black pepper or red pepper flakes to taste.

// Serve the hot stew over salad greens (lightly tossed with some olive oil, lemon juice, salt, and pepper). Sprinkle with more chopped parsley and red pepper flakes. Serve Dijon mustard on the side, if desired, to dollop on top. Toast slices of sourdough bread and rub them with the cut edge of the garlic clove, if desired, to eat alongside.

JULIE: On New Year's Eve a few years ago, right after Rusty and I moved into our new apartment and my youngest daughter, Sabine, was just twelve days old, I had the pleasure of first tasting this lentil stew. It was so deeply nourishing, and I was immediately taken back to winters in Minneapolis when I would regularly make a huge batch of lentils with loads of cumin and red pepper flakes and eat them daily to take the edge off how cold it was. Caroline's lentil stew warms me up in that same way. In place of the arugula, sometimes I wilt in fresh spinach and top it with red pepper flakes.

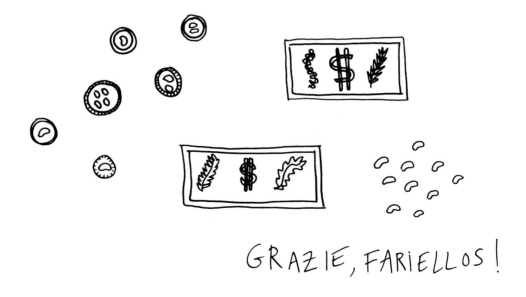

GRAZIE, FARIELLOS!

(pronounced sort of like hYOOguh)

HYGGE

// TINA

My Danish mom had a small Scandinavian store in Los Angeles, and our home was full of the household items that she couldn't bear to sell in the store, or that no one bought: bowls, broken Danish ceramics, candleholders, teapots, odd-looking clogs and mobiles. Equipped with just the right lighting and well-placed candles, our home was *hyggeligt*, Danish for "cozy." But here's the thing about the Danish word *hyggeligt*: It has many forms. You can *hygge* (verb) on a cold snowy day in front of the fire with hot tea and a good book. You can also *hygge* outside with some friends on a beautiful sunny day in the park with an ice-cold drink to cool you down. To *hygge* is to feel good. It captures that feeling you get when things are just right, either by chance or by intention. I can still hear my mom getting off the phone after catching up with an old friend and saying, "It was so nice to talk. *Det var rigtigt hyggeligt* [That was really cozy]." My mom and her Danish friends (who are now in their seventies and eighties and are still known collectively as "the girls") have birthdays and holiday parties where the spreads are thick with herring and aquavit and cold beer and rolls and pastry and good coffee and, of course, *smørrebrød*. It doesn't matter where the girls gather, in the backyard on a hot day, at a restaurant down by the beach for a birthday, or inside on a chilly evening. The girls make sure that these get-togethers are always *hyggelige*.

Enjoying soup is *hyggeligt,* whether hot or chilled, hearty or pureed, creamed or not, cooked at home and eaten with family, alone, or shared with friends. Soup Club is *Hygge* with a capital *H*.

Something like Mestemacher pumpernickel is a fine substitute for Danish rye bread, because it is thinly sliced and dense.

Smørrebrød are ubiquitous in Denmark. Kids' lunch boxes there are shaped to secure them in place, and with a sheet of wax paper on top of each layer, simple open-faced sandwiches do just fine: Examples are liver pâté with sliced cucumber on black bread, sliced potatoes with mayonnaise on rye bread, or sliced cheese under green pepper on rye bread.

In Danish, *smørrebrød* literally means buttered bread, and almost always, this is Danish rye bread, or *rugbrød*. But in practice, *smørrebrød* refers to bread with toppings, or *pålæg*. In English we call them open-faced sandwiches, because the toppings are on full display, making them beautiful, edible works of art. Like bagels with cream cheese, lox, onion, and tomato, *smørrebrød* is best when assembled at the table. Therefore, put them on the menu at your next brunch. You can assemble them or lay out some options and let your guests do it themselves. The variations are endless and anyone can add to the list. // TINA

SMØRREBRØD (DANISH OPEN-FACED SANDWICHES)

MAKES AS MUCH AS YOU NEED

FIVE VARIATIONS

1 // One hard-boiled egg thinly sliced (don't include the ends) and a dollop of mayonnaise on each slice of egg. Sprinkle with chopped chives. Dab caviar on top of each dollop of mayo.

2 // Two pieces of Havarti cheese topped with thinly sliced radish, green bell pepper, and alfalfa sprouts.

3 // Smoked salmon, dill sauce (recipe follows), dill sprig, and a slice of lemon.

4 // Thin egg omelet, cut to fit the bread. Top with curry mayonnaise (mix 1 teaspoon mayonnaise and curry powder to taste); red onion, quartered and thinly sliced; 2 small sardines or 1 large; and chopped chives.

5 // Three slices of herring, chopped red onion, and curry mayonnaise (see #4).

Garnish your *smørrebrød* by placing them on a leaf of butter lettuce.

Dill Sauce

MAKES ABOUT 1½ CUPS

In a small bowl, whisk together the mustards, vinegar, dill, salt, and oil. Use immediately or store in a glass jar with a tight-fitting lid. The sauce keeps well in the refrigerator for a couple of weeks.

6 teaspoons **honey mustard**

2 teaspoons **Dijon mustard**

2 tablespoons **vinegar**

½ cup finely minced fresh **dill**

Pinch of **salt**

⅔ cup neutral **oil**

I have never met anyone who makes their own applesauce and makes just enough for one meal. It really may be the foundational "Big Food" to share, so we thought this section was not complete without it. Applesauce was one of the first foods I made in bulk, passing off extra quarts for the freezer or the fridge to willing friends. When you're under the weather a warm bowl of applesauce can be a cold cure to rival chicken soup. It is an ideal side to a sandwich or roast (hello Porchetta-esque Pork Butt, page 206) and a perfect kid-tamer to serve while you cook. It also gives me good reason to use my trusty French food mill, and when it's simmering in the pot it makes the house smell amazing. The other thing about applesauce is that it is nearly impossible to screw up. You need nothing but apples and a bit of water; cinnamon if you want to be fancy. // **COURTNEY**

20 medium **apples**, washed, cored, and quartered, skins on

2 **cinnamon** sticks (optional)

Ground **cinnamon** (optional)

1 cup **Crème Fraîche** (page 47), optional

APPLESAUCE

MAKES 4 QUARTS

Pile all the apples in the stockpot. Add about 2 cups water, or enough to submerge about half the apples at the bottom of the pot.

// Cover and bring the water to a boil. Reduce the heat and simmer, covered, for 30 minutes, or until the apples begin to break down. Reduce the heat to low and stir every 20 minutes, adding water if needed so that the sauce doesn't burn. If using cinnamon sticks, add them after the first 40 minutes of cooking.

// The apples are done when they can be smashed against the side of the pot with a spoon. The sauce should remain lumpy. Turn off the heat and allow to cool to room temperature. Discard the cinnamon sticks, if using.

// Set the food mill over a large mixing bowl. (Placing the bowl on a damp dish towel will secure it in place.) Ladle the apple mixture into the mill 2 cups at a time, removing the peels as you go. Transfer the applesauce to glass jars with tight-fitting plastic freezer lids or to freezer zipper bags. Refrigerate or freeze immediately.

// To serve, warm the applesauce, if desired. Sprinkle with ground cinnamon or top with a dollop of crème fraîche.

FRENCH FOOD MILL

IF YOU DO NOT HAVE A FOOD MILL, peel the apples before cooking. The sauce will be paler in color because the skins, when milled, lend a rosy hue to the finished sauce. The experience of peeling 20 apples may prompt you to buy a food mill for your next batch of sauce. It is a good piece of equipment to own, as it makes great mashed potatoes, fruit purees, and silky sauces.

COOK'S SNACKS

Cooking soup makes you hungry. Inspiration for soup can turn into a snack like Korma-Spiced Nuts (page 235). Hummus (page 226) will appease the hungry vultures circling the kitchen. When you feel fancy, make Devils on Horseback (page 229)—because everything's better with bacon—and be on the lookout for a meal disguised as a snack, such as Potato Tortilla (page 228). Remember, saving the world through soup works up an appetite.

WATER CHESTNUT DIP

MAKES 2½ CUPS

Water chestnuts give this dip an unexpected and addictive crunch and soon you may find yourself slicing and even eating them right out of the can. Serve the dip with crudités. // COURTNEY

1 cup **mayonnaise**

1 cup **sour cream**

¼ cup chopped fresh **flat-leaf parsley** (leaves from 6 to 8 sprigs)

1 8-ounce can **water** chestnuts, drained and minced

1 tablespoon **soy sauce**

In a large bowl, combine the mayonnaise, sour cream, parsley, and water chestnuts. Add the soy sauce and stir to combine.

// This dip keeps, tightly covered, in the fridge for 2 days; stir before serving if it separates.

BABA GHANOUSH

MAKES 2 CUPS

This smoky, bright, and creamy dip is a must-make in the late summer and early fall when eggplant is in season. It can also be a condiment for meat or fish. Chef Yotam Ottolenghi's technique of laying the eggplant right on a gas burner is magic. No grill required.

Serve this with crudités, roasted vegetables (page 169), Crostini (page 179), or toasted pita wedges. // JULIE

2 large **eggplants**

4 to 6 tablespoons freshly squeezed **lemon juice** (from about 2 lemons)

3 tablespoons **tahini**

2 **garlic cloves**, crushed

2 tablespoons chopped fresh **mint**

2 tablespoons chopped fresh **flat-leaf parsley**

Salt and freshly ground **black pepper**

1 to 2 tablespoons **pomegranate seeds** (optional)

2 tablespoons **olive oil**

Using aluminum foil, line the area around two burners on a gas stove. Put the eggplants directly on the burners over a medium flame and turn occasionally with tongs. Char the eggplants for about 15 minutes, until they blacken and completely collapse. Allow to cool.

// Cut the eggplants lengthways and scoop out the flesh, discarding the skins. Put in a sieve and leave to drain in the sink or over a bowl for 30 minutes.

// Meanwhile, in a medium bowl, stir 4 tablespoons of the lemon juice into the tahini until it loosens up. Add up to 2 tablespoons more lemon juice if needed or to taste. Add the garlic and two thirds of the chopped herbs.

// Mash the eggplant flesh gently with a fork, and then stir it into the tahini mixture. Season with salt and pepper. Top with the remaining herbs and the pomegranate seeds, if using. Pour a moat of oil around the edge and serve. Store in the refrigerator, tightly covered, for up to a week.

CLASSIC HUMMUS

MAKES 5½ CUPS

> 3 15-ounce cans **chickpeas**, thoroughly rinsed, or
> 4½ cups cooked chickpeas
>
> 3 **garlic cloves**
>
> Zest and juice of 2 **lemons**
>
> ¾ cup **tahini**
>
> 1 teaspoon **salt**
>
> 6 tablespoons **olive oil**

Put the chickpeas, garlic, lemon zest and juice, tahini, and salt in a food processor. While processing, add the olive oil in a steady stream through the feed tube and blend for 2 minutes. Store in the refrigerator, covered, for up to a week.

TAHINI-LESS HUMMUS

MAKES 4½ CUPS

Caroline's son, Leo, really loved hummus, until he started getting hives from a tahini-sensitivity. I set out to make a tahini-free variation of my classic hummus that would taste just as good. Using a food processor is key here to whip either variation until creamy and smooth. // COURTNEY

> 3 15-ounce cans **chickpeas**, thoroughly rinsed, or
> 4½ cups cooked **chickpeas**
>
> 3 **garlic cloves**
>
> Grated zest and juice of 2 **lemons**
>
> 1 teaspoon **salt**
>
> ¾ cup **olive oil**

Put the chickpeas, garlic, lemon zest and juice, and salt in a food processor. While processing, add the olive oil in a steady stream through the feed tube until combined, then blend for 2 minutes. This may seem like a long time, but that's what gives the hummus its lightness. Store in the refrigerator, covered, for up to a week.

GARLIC HERBED CHEESE

MAKES 1¼ CUPS

Seriously, don't even think of using fresh herbs in this. It won't be the same. Dried herbs keep the cream cheese and butter creamy white and resist total pulverization in the food processor. // COURTNEY

> 1 8-ounce package **cream cheese**, at room
> temperature
>
> 8 tablespoons (1 stick) unsalted **butter**, at room
> temperature
>
> 1 teaspoon dried **tarragon**
>
> 1 teaspoon dried **parsley**
>
> 1 teaspoon dried **chives**
>
> 2 **garlic cloves**, minced
>
> ½ teaspoon **salt**, plus more if needed

Combine the cream cheese, butter, herbs, garlic, and salt in a food processor until well blended. Adjust the salt if needed. Transfer to a crock or other serving container and refrigerate for at least 1 hour, or until ready to serve. This will keep for 10 days, tightly covered, in the refrigerator.

Ramp Two Ways

(AND MARITAL COMPROMISE)

Dear Ian,

You are my first and most appreciative taster of soups and more. I know you wish our lives had slightly less kale and a lot more foie gras, but since that equation (let's be honest) will never tip in your favor, instead I dedicate all the ramps to you. And not only the ramps, but also the garlic scapes, garlic shoots, leeks, chives, scallions—all those allium-family babies that you love so much. I will keep on devising ways for us to eat them.

Love, Caroline

RAMP-CHOVY PASTE

MAKES ABOUT 2 CUPS

Not for the faint of heart. // CAROLINE

2 bunches **ramps**, stringy roots removed
1 cup chopped **walnuts**, toasted (see page 000)
1 small (2-ounce) tin **oil-packed anchovies**
¼ to ½ cup **olive oil**

Combine the ramps, walnuts, anchovies and their oil, and ¼ cup of the olive oil in a food processor and pulse until smooth. The anchovies (and their funky oil) should take care of saltiness.

SERVING IDEAS: *Combine equal parts ramp-chovy paste and mayonnaise for special deviled eggs. Schmear on simple roasted fish, add to Amanda's Grilled Cheese Croutons (page 43), and spread on Crostini (page 179).*

RAMPS are in the onion family and look like scallions going out to a party. They're in season in the Northeast for just a few weeks in spring. If ramps aren't available, scallions, scapes, chives, and baby leeks can substitute.

WHITE BEAN–RAMP–RADISH MASH

MAKES ABOUT 4 CUPS

Serve as a dip with tortilla chips or as a filling for small, soft, corn taco shells. // CAROLINE

6 tablespoons **olive oil**
1 bunch **ramps**, stringy roots removed and thinly sliced
3 cups cooked **white beans** (or use 2 15-ounce cans of white beans, drained and rinsed)
8 to 10 large **radishes**, stem and roots removed, thinly sliced into half-moons
Salt and freshly ground **black pepper**

Heat 2 tablespoons of the oil in a large cast-iron pan and add the ramps. Cook over medium heat, stirring occasionally, until the ramps are wilted.

// Add the beans to the pan and as they heat up, mash them with the back of a spatula or spoon. (Alternately, don't mash the beans at all, and serve this as a warm salad.) Keep stirring as you mash, to combine the beans and ramps, and drizzle in 2 more tablespoons of the oil (the beans really soak it up).

// Add the radishes, stir to combine, and press the whole mash down into the bottom of the pan. Let it sit there, untouched, for another minute, and remove from the heat. Drizzle over the remaining 2 tablespoons of olive oil just before serving. Serve warm or at room temperature. Store, covered, in the refrigerator for up to three days.

POTATO TORTILLA

SERVES 8 *PARA PICAR* (AS AN APPETIZER)

Omelets are my dad's Sunday brunch specialty, and I've always been drawn to variations of beaten eggs in a hot pan. When I lived in Madrid years ago, my lovely Spanish teacher said that it was essential I learn how to make a Spanish tortilla (an egg-in-pan tapa) and took me through it step by step. There is a bit of technique here that gets easier with practice. Keep your wits about you and don't be alarmed by the amount of olive oil in the recipe. It's just the way it's done. // JULIE

> 3 medium **Yukon Gold potatoes** (about 1½ pounds), peeled
>
> **Salt**
>
> 1¼ cups **olive oil**
>
> 1 medium **onion**, diced
>
> 3 **garlic cloves**, minced
>
> 6 large **eggs**
>
> Chopped fresh **flat-leaf parsley** (optional)
>
> Freshly ground **black pepper**

Slice the potatoes as thin as you can. You can also use a mandoline set to ⅛ inch thick. Pat the potato slices completely dry and season liberally with salt. Be sure to do this immediately before cooking, otherwise the salt will bring out more moisture and discolor the potatoes.

// Heat the oil in a heavy 9- to 10-inch skillet (preferably nonstick) over medium-high heat until very hot, about 3 minutes. Reduce the heat to medium low and add the potato slices in even layers. Cook for about 8 minutes, or until the potatoes are about half cooked, turning occasionally to prevent the potatoes from sticking.

// Stir in the onions and garlic, reduce the heat to low, and cook the mixture for another 15 minutes, turning occasionally, or until the potatoes are soft. Using a slotted spoon, transfer the potato mixture to a colander set over a bowl and drain thoroughly. Strain and set aside the cooking oil.

// In a large mixing bowl, whisk the eggs until just combined. Add the potato mixture and gently break up the pieces a bit with a fork.

// Heat 3 tablespoons of the reserved oil in the skillet over medium-high heat. Pour the egg and potato mixture into the skillet and flatten the top with a spatula.

// Reduce the heat to medium low and while the tortilla is cooking, shake the skillet a bit and run a thin spatula around the edge to allow the egg mixture to cook evenly. After a minute or two, cook without disturbing until the tortilla is mostly set and the top is slightly wet but not uncooked, 6 to 8 minutes. Run the spatula around the edges again and along the bottom of the tortilla to ensure it's not sticking.

// Top the skillet with a plate slightly larger than the skillet, and using oven mitts, quickly invert the tortilla over the plate. Add a tablespoon or two more of the reserved olive oil to the skillet and carefully slide the tortilla back into the skillet. Reduce the heat to low and cook until an inserted toothpick comes out clean, 3 to 4 minutes.

// Invert the tortilla onto a serving plate and pat the top of the tortilla with a paper towel to remove excess oil.

// Let cool a little and then slice the tortilla into pie-shaped wedges or tiny squares. Sprinkle chopped parsley over the top, if desired. Season with salt and pepper. Serve warm or at room temperature.

Q. What is vegan, gluten-free, a childhood favorite, and a crowd-pleaser?

A. **ANTS ON A LOG**, of course, a never-fail offering.

Traditionally, it's peanut butter schmeared into the groove of a celery stick, topped off by raisins. For me, it's a perfect food combination: cool and crunchy, salty-creamy, sweet and chewy, all in one handheld bite. I served them at the first Oscar party Ian and I cohosted, and I served them at our most recent Oscar party. The tray is always greeted with lots of laughs, and I always find myself back in the kitchen to prep second or third rounds.

   With decades of experience in the eating and making of Ants on a Log under my belt, I have several personal commandments that I follow every time, sort of like a recipe. // CAROLINE

// *The celery* has to be dried really, really well. Get into the grooves with a clean paper towel, or else you're setting yourself up for watery peanut butter. Cut each stalk into three pieces.

// *The peanut butter* has to have only two ingredients: peanuts and salt. The saltier the better.

// *The raisins* have to be dark and chewy. Meaning not golden, and not from an opened, half-eaten package from some forgotten era.

GROWN-UP ANTS ON A LOG

Instead of raisins, substitute a dab of medium-spicy mango chutney. Add a few sprinkles of red pepper flakes.

DEVILS ON HORSEBACK

SERVES 8 TO 10

This is a great alcohol absorber. // CAROLINE

- ½ pound creamy, sharp **blue cheese**, such as Bleu d'Auvergne, at room temperature
- 32 extra-large **dates**, figs, or prunes (or a combination), pitted
- 16 slices (standard, not thick) best-quality **bacon** (about 1 pound), cut in half

Preheat the oven to 350°F.

   // Break off a bit of cheese, and force it into a date. (This is why you want a creamy blue. Crumbly blue is a huge mess.) Repeat with the remaining cheese and dates.

   // Wrap a half slice of bacon around each date. Secure with a toothpick. Lay the wrapped dates on a foil-lined rimmed baking sheet and bake for 15 minutes, or until the bacon is cooked. Set on a paper-towel-lined plate to drain excess grease. Serve while still warm.

Vegetarian option

Omit the bacon. Cut a few radicchio leaves into long, thick ribbons. Brush them with olive oil and wrap around the dates. Sprinkle with kosher salt before baking. Bake for 5 minutes.

Vegan option

Substitute almond butter for the blue cheese and omit the bacon. Wrap the stuffed dates with the radicchio and bake for 5 minutes.

MELTED CHEESE CRACKERS

MAKES 24 CRACKERS

Sliced Cracker Barrel mild cheddar and Triscuits, eaten in front of the television, were a staple of my childhood. I recommend a hearty wheat cracker to accompany a sharp melted cheese, but any combination works. I have been known to make a meal of these after a long day (glass of red wine not optional). // COURTNEY

24 hearty **wheat crackers**

6 ounces **medium-sharp cheddar cheese**, sliced in ¼-inch-thick pieces the same size as the crackers

1 small bunch **chives**

Set the broiler to high and move an oven rack to the middle position.

// Arrange the crackers on a foil-lined rimmed baking sheet so they are not touching. Place 1 piece of cheese on each cracker, taking care that the cheese doesn't hang over the cracker edge.

// Broil for 2 to 3 minutes, until the cheese is melted and just starting to bubble. Remove the tray from the oven and transfer the crackers to a serving platter. Snip the chives over the crackers so that each cracker gets a confetti-like treatment for color and flavor. Serve immediately.

HONEY, RICOTTA, AND BLACK PEPPER BRUSCHETTA

MAKES APPROXIMATELY 32 BRUSCHETTA

Once, I signed myself up for a class with Betsy Devine and Rachel Marks of Salvatore Bklyn, an artisan cheese company in Brooklyn. They led twenty cheese geeks through the relatively simple process of making ricotta from scratch, making the process look both fun and easy. I have made ricotta exactly zero times since the class, but I have eaten Salvatore Bklyn's ricotta nearly every week. If you can get your hands on some, I recommend experimenting with both the regular and the smoky varieties. The texture of fresh ricotta is close to that of cream cheese and is perfect for spreading on crostini. If you are using grocery store ricotta, have no fear. This is still an unexpected and crave-inducing combination. // COURTNEY

1 recipe **Crostini** (page 179)

8 ounces good-quality **ricotta**

¼ cup **honey**

1 teaspoon large-flake **sea salt**, such as Maldon

Freshly ground **black pepper**

Spread each piece of crostini with 1½ teaspoons of the ricotta. Drizzle with honey, sprinkle with salt, and add a generous grind of pepper. Eat immediately.

SWEET AND SPICY NUTS

Makes 8 cups

These are party nuts; they have complemented many a karaoke adventure. But they also have fueled many late working nights. My first encounter with fancy nuts was at a fancy hotel bar in Chicago, where my father treated me to my first martini while I was home from freshman year of college (not quite of age, but don't tell). He wasn't a ritual-heavy kind of guy, but he thought I needed the right introduction to proper cocktails. // CAROLINE

> 2 teaspoons ground **cinnamon**
>
> 2 teaspoons ground **cumin**
>
> 2 teaspoons cayenne **pepper**
>
> 1 teaspoon ground **allspice**
>
> 1 teaspoon ground **ginger**
>
> ½ to ¾ cup **turbinado sugar** or **granulated sugar**, depending on how sweet you like it
>
> 4 teaspoons **salt**
>
> 2 **egg whites** (use the yolks for Black Olive Shortbread, page 191, or Caesar Dressing, page 154), plus more if needed to coat nuts completely
>
> 2 pounds mixed **raw nuts** (such as cashews, almonds, pecan halves, peanuts, and hazelnuts)

Preheat the oven to 250°F.

// Combine the spices, sugar, and salt in a small bowl.

// In a large bowl, beat the egg whites until very foamy but not stiff and add the nuts, stirring to coat. Add the spice mixture to the nuts and stir to combine.

// Spread the nuts evenly in a single layer on 2 ungreased rimmed baking sheets and bake for 1 hour, stirring every 20 minutes. After the first 20 minutes, check the taste and sprinkle on extra salt or sugar if desired. Switch the position of the two baking sheets midway, to prevent uneven baking. Remove the pans from the oven and let the nuts cool completely.

CINNAMON-SUGAR WALNUTS

MAKES 8 CUPS

These follow the same technique as the Sweet and Spicy Nuts, at left, but have a friendly, simpler sweetness. You can omit or reduce the cayenne pepper, but that kick of spice complements the cinnamon-sugar. For some reason, this is best with craggy walnuts, though pecans can substitute. Serve as a premeal snack or with one of the pureed soups—Chestnut (page 78), Carrot Coconut (page 75), or Roasted Parsnip (page 85)—or even with Moroccan Coriander Vegetable Soup (page 102). // CAROLINE

> 1½ cups **sugar**
>
> 4 teaspoons **salt**
>
> 4 teaspoons ground **cinnamon**
>
> 2 teaspoons cayenne **pepper**
>
> 2 **egg whites**
>
> 2 pounds raw **walnut** or **pecans halves**

Preheat the oven to 250°F.

// Combine the sugar, salt, cinnamon, and cayenne pepper in a small bowl.

// In a large bowl, beat the egg whites until very foamy but not stiff and add the nuts, stirring to coat. Add the sugar mixture and stir to combine.

// Spread the nuts evenly in a single layer on two ungreased rimmed baking sheets and bake for 1 hour, stirring every 20 minutes. Switch the position of the two baking sheets midway, to prevent uneven baking. Remove the pans from the oven and let the nuts cool completely.

KORMA-SPICED NUTS

MAKES 8 CUPS

These nuts are the happy offspring of my Cauliflower Korma on page 107; I had some extra spice blend left over after making that soup and I devised this roasted vegan nut concoction from that surplus. This flavorful blend of nuts is a great stand-alone snack, and it also presents well if you need to whip up a quick batch for office or school gifts, or even for a friend's birthday party at the local bar. Be sure to offer some to the bartender. // TINA

- ½ teaspoon ground **cardamom**
- 1 tablespoon ground **turmeric**
- 1 teaspoon **red pepper flakes**, or to taste
- 1 tablespoon ground **cumin**
- 1 tablespoon ground **coriander**
- 1 teaspoon ground **cinnamon**
- ⅛ teaspoon freshly ground black **pepper**
- 2 pounds mixed **raw nuts** (such as almonds, cashews, pecan halves, and hazelnuts)
- ½ cup pure **maple syrup**
- 1 tablespoon **neutral oil**
- 2 teaspoons **salt**, plus more to taste
- 2 cups unsweetened **coconut chips** (which are larger than flakes) or flaked coconut (if you can't find chips)

Preheat the oven to 275°F. Place the oven racks in the upper third and lower third of the oven. Line two rimmed baking sheets with parchment paper.

// In a large bowl, mix the spices, nuts, maple syrup, oil, salt, and coconut chips until well incorporated. Spread the mixture evenly in a single layer on the baking sheets.

// Bake without stirring for about 50 minutes, or until the edges of the coconut chips or flakes are just starting to brown. Switch the position of the two baking sheets midway, to prevent uneven baking.

// Remove the pans from the oven and let the nuts cool completely. The nuts will be in clumps; de-clump according to preference. (I like clumps.)

ALMONDS WITH ROSEMARY

MAKES 6 TO 8 CUPS

Rosemary works well with these Spanish-inspired nuts, but play with the herbs or add spice, such as red pepper flakes or cayenne pepper, if you like. Perfectly content to stand alone, these nuts also pair nicely with Chickpea, Roasted Squash, and Farro Soup (page 67). // JULIE

- ¼ cup chopped fresh **rosemary leaves**
- ⅓ cup **olive oil**
- 1½ teaspoons **salt**
- 2 pounds raw **almonds**, whole or slivered

Preheat the oven to 325°F.

// In a large bowl, mix the rosemary with the oil and salt. Toss in the almonds and evenly coat with the olive oil mixture.

// Spread the almonds evenly in a single layer on two ungreased rimmed baking sheets and bake for 5 minutes. Stir and bake for 10 to 12 more minutes, or until the almonds are nicely browned and fragrant and the herbs are crisp. If using slivered almonds, start checking for doneness after 5 minutes. They burn more quickly that their whole counterpart. Remove from the oven and allow to cool to room temperature.

ACKNOWLEDGMENTS

We are four friends who cook, but we wouldn't be Soup Club without the vital and much-loved gravitational forces that brought us together and keep us in orbit.

Our kids, for their relentless need to eat and play (at regular and irregular intervals), and for almost always trying our soups: Eleanor and Edwin; Nico, Oscar, and Cleo; Alice and Leo; Isabel, Dashiel, and Sabine.

To Sam, forever.

Our families, immediate and extended. We wouldn't be who we are without our moms (to whom this book is also dedicated), dads (Joel and Tim), brothers (Kevin and Tom), and sisters (Kim, Stephanie, and Sara). And Tom and Bob, the loved dads who are no longer with us.

Our editor, Doris Cooper, without whom the book wouldn't exist. Your unmatched enthusiasm, warmth, talent, and expertise saw us through a long winter of rewriting and cooking. Thank you for guiding four novices and supporting our vision. We are so very grateful. Our agent, Daniel Greenberg, who enjoyed Soup Club first-hand. You saw this as a cookbook before any of us and found us the perfect home. You were right about everything.

To the incredibly gifted Clarkson Potter team, especially Jane Treuhaft, Laura Palese, Emma Brodie, Mark McCauslin, Phil Leung, Anna Mintz, and Carly Gorga. And big thanks to Pam Krauss for believing in this book from the beginning.

Annie Schlechter and Kate Neckel, you are masters of your art.

To our photography team, Khalil, Dylan, and Mrs. A. Your tireless attention to detail is inspiring.

To Global Master Cutlery, Le Creuset, and Judy at Weck Jars for providing us with a wealth of soup tools. To Sarah Abrams and Adeena Sussman, for testing our giant recipes. To our cherished local shop owners. Your first-rate food stuffs and merchandise have fueled us for years and inspire our cooking: Grand Street CSA; Shahin of Dual Specialty Store; Essex Street Market, including Formaggio and Essex Farm, and with special thanks to Anne of Saxelby Cheesemongers and Patrick of Heritage Meats; Ammar Ajaz and M. Shafiq of Lahore Deli, this book was written on the strength of your chai; Michael of Lost Weekend NYC; Malt & Mold; The Pickle Guys; Russ & Daughters; September Wines; Atef of SOS Chefs; and The Sweet Life.

To our neighbors on Grand Street, an amazing small village in the middle of a very large city. We truly love our shared community and appreciate you every day.

To our generous donors of time, energy, and good advice: Syd Butler, Amy Carlson, Shien Chiou, Amanda Cohen, Rachel Fershleiser, Sarah Gephart, Andy Goldman, Carlin Greenstein, Sarah Huck, Carly Jacobs, Ingrid Katz, Linda Monastra, Lauren Pilgrim, Katya Rogers, Ian Rosenberg, Eddie Stern, and Alexi Wright.

To our friends near and far, who have shaped our biographies and given us stories to share. We appreciate your enduring interest in soup (which, okay, isn't always that interesting).

To soup-eating mammals everywhere.

And finally, to our partners in love and soup: David, Dan, Ian and Rusty.

INDEX

Note: Page references in *italics* indicate photographs.